I0890239

Charter Schools against the Odds

EDUCATION next
BOOKS

gratefully acknowledges the following individuals and foundations for support of this research

LYNDE AND HARRY BRADLEY FOUNDATION

JERRY AND PATTI HUME

KORET FOUNDATION

BERNARD AND CATHERINE SCHWARTZ FOUNDATION

WILLIAM E. SIMON FOUNDATION

BOYD AND JILL SMITH

TAD AND DIANNE TAUBE FOUNDATION

JACK AND MARY LOIS WHEATLEY

An Assessment by the Hoover Institution's Koret Task Force on K–12 Education

Charter Schools against the Odds

Edited by
Paul T. Hill

Contributions by
John E. Chubb
Chester E. Finn Jr.
Paul T. Hill
Caroline M. Hoxby
Eric Osberg
Paul E. Peterson
Brad Smith
Nathan Torinus

EDUCATION next
BOOKS
Stanford University
Stanford, California

The Hoover Institution on War, Revolution and Peace, founded at Stanford University in 1919 by Herbert Hoover, who went on to become the thirty-first president of the United States, is an interdisciplinary research center for advanced study on domestic and international affairs. The views expressed in its publications are entirely those of the authors and do not necessarily reflect the views of the staff, officers, or Board of Overseers of the Hoover Institution.

www.hoover.org

EDUCATION next BOOKS

An imprint of the Hoover Institution Press

Hoover Institution Press Publication No. 549

First printing, 2006
13 12 11 10 09 08 07 06 9 8 7 6 5 4 3 2 1

Manufactured in the United States of America

The paper used in this publication meets the minimum requirements of the American National Standard for Information Sciences—Permanence of Paper for Printed Library Materials, ANSI Z39.48-1992. ♾

Library of Congress Cataloging-in-Publication Data
Charter schools against the odds / edited by Paul T. Hill.
p. cm. — (Hoover Institution Press publication ; no. 549)
Includes bibliographical references and index.
ISBN 0-8179-4761-2 (alk. paper) — ISBN 0-8179-4762-0 (pbk. : alk. paper)
1. Charter schools—Government policy—United States. I. Hill, Paul Thomas, 1943– II. Series: Hoover Institution Press publication ; 549.
LB2806.36.C536 2006
371.01—dc22 2006008873

Contents

Introduction

Paul T. Hill

Charter schools were born into a hostile environment. For some, they represented an exciting vehicle of school reform; for others, especially those in control of the current public school system, they were a threat.

Charter schools are publicly funded schools operated by independent groups under contract with government agencies. They provide an alternative to traditional public schools, which are all operated by bureaucratically organized school districts. Charter schools are based on freedom of action and choice. Individual schools can use different teaching methods than the surrounding public schools and make innovative use of time, technology, and money. No teacher can be assigned to work in a charter school—schools employ teachers by mutual consent—and no child can be required to attend a charter school.

The first charter schools opened in Minnesota in 1992, but by 2006 they had spread to forty-one states. There are now 3900 charter schools serving nearly a million students—large numbers given how recently the first charter schools emerged and, as we shall see, the ferocity of opposition they generate. But chartering is still a relatively small element of the nation's public education system, which educates twenty million students in over 100,000 schools.[1]

Some state laws make it easy for a group with a new idea to get a charter, while others erect major barriers. Some state laws emphasize creation of charter schools in urban areas and encourage schools to serve poor and disadvantaged students who need options, but others do not. Consequently, charter schools serve disproportionately disadvantaged populations in most states, but not all.

Everyone wants to know, are charter schools working?[2] And there is an answer: yes, some are, based on the learning rates of students who attend them, but some aren't. Their performance depends on a lot of things including whether they receive as much money as other public schools in their communities or must do with a lot less, and whether they have had enough time for teachers and administrators to learn to work together efficiently. It is very hard to draw generalizations across states with different charter laws, and to reach a bottom-line judgment on a movement whose schools are mostly new. Charter schools also offer an inviting target to critics who can find one or two bad ones to complain about. Though it is unreasonable to expect every charter school to be effective the day it opens (especially in urban areas where half or more of the district-run schools are labeled low performing) opponents are quick to turn localized problems into

1. For rich information about the charter school movement see Greg Vanourek, *The State of the Charter Movement 2005* (Washington DC: National Alliance for Public Charter Schools, 2005), and Robin J. Lake, et al., *Hopes Fears and Reality: A Balanced Look at Charter Schools in 2005* (Seattle: National Charter School Research Project, 2005).

2. For a review of evidence on charter performance, see Charter School Achievement Consensus Panel, *Key Issues for Studying Charter Schools and Achievement, a Review and Suggestions for National Guidelines* (Seattle: National Charter School Research Project, 2006).

indictments of charter schools in general. Unlike district-run schools, bad charter schools eventually disappear and new ones take their place. Even if the average quality of charter schools becomes very high, there will always be some that struggle and might soon close.

Even before definite bottom-line conclusions about charter schools in general can be drawn, some things are evident. The charter movement is alive and well, but facing some serious challenges. Like humans at the age of twenty, the charter school movement is vibrant and promising, but no one can be sure exactly what sort of adult will eventually emerge.

Many of the charter movement's problems are endemic to what it is trying to do. It is not easy to start new schools. New schools must make a functioning team out of adults gathered from diverse places and different experiences. They must define a coherent approach to teaching and learning, so that families know what their children will experience in the classroom and potential teachers will know whether the school is the right place for them. They must figure out how to judge their own performance and when necessary make changes, even in instructional methods that originally defined the school. In addition, a lot of things taken for granted in existing schools must be established from scratch, including basic arrangements for paying the bills, hiring people, attracting customers, and taking care of buildings and grounds.

All these challenges have proven difficult, and many charter schools are taking longer than anyone expected to jell as educational institutions. This is true in part because the school start-up process was poorly understood before large numbers of charter schools started to go through it. Though school districts had started thousands of schools, the fact that they did not have to attract parents and teachers who could choose to go elsewhere meant that nobody paid much attention to their start-up problems.

"Jelling" problems are also rooted in widespread high hopes about charter schools. Thousands of parents and educators had longed for an opportunity to realize their vision of a good school. Often, people with different visions found themselves together in one school. Working out the conflicts in vision, even to the point of separating into different schools, takes time.

The charter movement has other problems, however, that are not related to the challenges of starting schools. The state laws that allow charter schools to exist can also make it very hard for them to succeed. Charter schools must compete with district-run public schools for students and teachers, but the competition takes place on a decidedly un-level playing field. Most state laws give charter schools less money per pupil than districts get, and require charter schools to pay for important things that district-run schools get free, starting with the buildings they occupy. Charter schools also bear the burden of proof when they seek permission to enroll students and receive funds, and in most states they must be re-authorized every three to five years.

This book focuses on ways state laws create an un-level playing field and suggests how state laws and policies can be amended to give charter schools—and the children they serve—a fairer chance to succeed.

How the Playing Field Was Tilted against Charter Schools

Charter school laws are strongly affected by legislative process. Though the forty-one charter school laws are highly diverse, one thing is true about how they were enacted: only a handful were rammed through the legislature as part of a powerful governor's defined legislative package. Instead, the vast majority were enacted through the efforts of legislative entrepreneurs who had to make many deals and overcome powerful opposition in order to gain votes for passage.

The un-level playing field was built through the legislative bargaining process. Like so many issues that come before legislatures, charter schools had some strong proponents and some opponents, but many legislators were indifferent or nearly so. To get the laws enacted, proponents had to seek votes by making strong claims about how much charter schools would produce and how little they would cost. They also had to assuage the fears of others who were not opposed to charter schools but wanted to make sure key constituencies were protected. At the same time, entrenched opponents supported by teacher union and school board lobbies fought against charter schools and called in political debts to get votes from uncommitted legislators.

School board associations were concerned that competition from charters could take funds away from their school districts, and that board members would be held responsible for the performance of schools they did not control. Teachers' unions feared that growth of charter schools would shrink public school districts and reduce the numbers of jobs available for unionized teachers. Unions also feared that charters would be popular with parents and teachers, leading to demands for schooling arrangements incompatible with teacher collective bargaining agreements.

The need to reassure potential swing voters—who might be willing to vote for charter schools but were also concerned about school boards' and unions' fears—often led proponents to accept provisions that tilted the playing field against charter schools. Relevant provisions can be combined into two loose categories: those sponsored by opponents who preferred to stop charter schools entirely but were forced to accept them in some form, and those introduced by proponents in order to attract swing votes by making the costs seem low and the benefits seem high.

Provisions Introduced by Opponents

Field-tilting provisions encouraged by opponents were the more numerous. In many states, only school districts—which generally opposed charter schools—were allowed to grant charters. Moreover, laws often did not require districts to consider charter proposals at all, or set the standards to use in evaluating proposals if they chose to do so. In states where chartering is left entirely to the discretion of school districts, new charter schools are relatively rare. In Illinois, for example, only Chicago has been open to chartering, and most other districts in the state have rejected all charter applications put before them. Some laws gave school districts a fig leaf—the opportunity to grant charters to some of their existing schools—considered much less threatening than new schools that brought new talent and money into public education.

The picture is very different in states where proponents were able to win multiple routes to chartering—via appeal to the state if a local district arbitrarily rejects charter applications, and if not through the local district, then to another possible authorizer including a state college, mayor's office, or nonprofit. In states with such provisions the charter movement starts more schools, offers more varied options, and serves more children.

Opponents also won restrictive caps on the numbers of charter schools allowed in a state. Caps were set so low in many cases—fifteen in Illinois, twenty-five in Massachusetts—that school districts were exposed to very little financial risk and were unlikely to experience the pressure of competition. When caps keep the numbers of charter schools low, they make it difficult for schools to share expertise, join risk sharing pools to pay for unexpected costs of special education, and develop active constituencies of families that want the choices charter schools provide. Caps also discourage private firms from developing lines of business providing services—payroll, insurance, lending, employee benefits, and facilities maintenance—that charter schools need.

Opponents also tried to make sure charter schools were isolated one-off institutions, by forbidding for-profit firms from holding charters. This insulated school districts from a kind of competition they feared—for-profit firms able to use investment capital to make major financial investments in their school designs and eager to expand rapidly to exploit economies of scale.

Teacher unions won their own protections at charter schools' expense, in the form of provisions that limit the time a unionized teacher can work in a charter school without losing seniority rights. These arrangements force experienced teachers to choose between working in charter schools and enjoying the benefits they have earned through seniority, and thereby reduce charter schools' access to qualified staff.

Finally, provisions that force charter schools to pay rent out of operating funds put them at a financial disadvantage *vis a vis* district-run schools. Further, requirements that charter schools must pay for services that district schools get free—from health screening to student transportation and teacher training—deepens charter schools' financial disadvantage.

Provisions Introduced by Proponents

Three kinds of legislative provision are compromises made by charter supporters to attract votes. Compromises were necessary; the alternative was no charter law at all. But the compromises had practical consequences, often serious.

The first important compromise was limited funding, often as little as 75 percent of the money school districts would get to educate the same students. This tilts the playing field because charter schools must buy goods and services and hire staff in the same market as local district-run schools. Lack of money has particularly adverse implications for teacher hiring. Less money means charter schools cannot offer the same total pay and benefits packages as the district-run schools with which they most compete for students. Though charter school teaching is an attractive job for young college graduates on a mission, these individuals turn over quickly as they pursue graduate studies or pursue other missions. Meanwhile, older teachers who pay mortgages and support families must make rational economic calculations. It is hard for charter schools to get and keep such teachers.

The second compromise is limited charter terms. Proponents could tell worried legislatures, "a charter's term lasts only five (or in some states three) years, and after that if the government agency that approved the charter doesn't like it, the school must go away." However, this arrangement has had negative effects on charter schools. Because they are ensured of existing for only a short time, and the basis on which renewal decisions will be made is not always clear, charter schools have difficulty borrowing money and entering desirable long-term leases for facilities. The fixed charter term has also discouraged many school districts and other government agencies from developing a capacity to oversee charter school performance. Instead, some agencies ignore charter schools unless scandals arise, waiting to assess the balance of political support and opposition for a school when its charter comes up for renewal. This changes the basis of charter school accountability, substituting political calculation for assessment of student learning effects.

The third compromise is charter laws' silence about the duties of school districts and other state agencies designated by law to grant charters. Rather than clarify the duties of authorizers, proponents avoided firing up school districts' opposition by saying nothing about the standards by which charter proposals should be judged, authorizers' responsibilities for ongoing oversight, or what should be done about low-performing charter schools. Consequently, authorizers were left to define their own responsibilities. Though some thought hard about what it meant to hold schools accountable for performance, not compliance, most did not. Some authorizers granted charters and then ignored the schools entirely, leading to preventable disasters in cases of schools that had never developed the basic capacity to manage instruction. Under such authorizers, even the most conscientious charter school leaders did not know for what they would be held accountable.

Once it was possible to assemble enough votes for passage of a charter school law, even one with many problems, proponents had a strong incentive to press for a vote before other issues might cause new controversies. Thus, a great number of questions were left to administrators and school districts to resolve. These included charter schools' access to publicly owned school buildings, rights to special education services for their students, teachers' access to publicly funded pension plans, and claims to services—like transportation and payroll—that school districts normally provide free to public schools.

In practice, these issues were virtually all resolved to charter schools' disadvantage. In most states, charter schools not only received less money per pupil than school districts spend on their own pupils; they also had to pay for things that district-run pubic schools did not. This included facilities, which district-run schools receive free and are built and maintained from separate capital accounts, not district operating funds, and pensions, for which districts normally receive off the books state subsidies.

Table I.1 illustrates how some of the key provisions that tilt the playing field against charter schools are distributed by state. The table presents a harsh picture. As this is written more than half the states with charter schools have caps that limit or rule out increases in the numbers of charter schools. Of states with

Table I.1 Supply-Limiting Elements in State Charter Laws (bullets indicate elements that tilt the playing field against charter schools)

State	*Caps Severely Limiting Growth*	*Only District May Authorize*	*Less than Full Per-Pupil Funding*	*No For-Profit Charter Holders*
Alaska		•	•	•
Arizona			•	
Arkansas	•		•	•
California			•	•
Colorado			•	
Connecticut		•	•	•
Delaware				•
D.C.				•
Florida				•
Georgia		•	•	•
Hawaii	•		•	•
Idaho	•	•	•	•
Illinois	•	•	•	•
Indiana	•	•		•
Iowa	•	•		•
Kansas		•	•	•
Louisiana	•	•	•	•
Maryland				•
Massachusetts	•			
Michigan	•			•
Minnesota			•	•
Mississippi	•	•		•
Missouri	•		•	•
Nevada	•	•		•
New Hampshire	•		•	•
New Jersey			•	•
New Mexico		•		•
New York	•		•	•
North Carolina	•			•
Ohio	•		•	•
Oklahoma		•		•
Oregon		•	•	•
Pennsylvania		•		•
Rhode Island	•		•	•
South Carolina			•	•
Tennessee	•	•		•
Texas	•		•	•
Utah	•			•
Virginia		•		
Wisconsin	•			
Wyoming		•	•	•

caps only California still allows room for large numbers of new schools (360)—and even that cap is much too low to allow charter schools to enroll a major share of the state's students. Districts can still keep a stranglehold on chartering in eighteen states, and the majority of states provide less money for a student in a charter school than in a district-run school. Only four states allow for-profit organizations to hold charters.

As this book documents, however, many charter schools have found ways to fight their way uphill. Schools have coped by improvising, relying on contributed time and money, avoiding the most hostile environments, and taking risks when the needs of children required it. Some schools have also failed at these things.

Charter proponents, including elected officials, philanthropists, and new pro-charter associations, have continued trying to improve charter laws, by lifting caps and creating more equitable funding and regulatory arrangements. However, charter opponents have also remained active, working to hold down the numbers of laws and imposing new regulations whenever a problem in an individual charter school gives them an opening to do so. Teachers unions have also tried to erode charter schools' freedom to hire teachers on the basis of fit, via efforts, generally unsuccessful to date, to organize charter school teachers.

This Book

Succeeding chapters will discuss ways in which adverse provisions of law and policy create problems for charter schools, and how charter schools have survived and served families well, against the odds. A final chapter will suggest how charter schools can be strengthened by a combination of changes in state law, public investments in performance-based school oversight, and private initiatives supported by philanthropy.

In chapter 1, Caroline M. Hoxby provides empirical evidence

about how legislative provisions affect the numbers of charter schools that emerge. She shows that the supply of charter schools is highly elastic, i.e. that it responds strongly to elements of state law like the funding available to charter schools and the degree to which charters control their hiring, spending, and instructional programs. Hostile or inequitable laws suppress the supply of charter schools, and laws offering a more truly level playing field encourage formation of many strong charter schools.

In chapter 2, Eric Osberg provides an overview of charter school funding and costs. He shows how charter school funding falls short of the amounts available to public school districts, and how the extra costs they must bear puts charter schools at a further financial disadvantage. Osberg considers the value of philanthropy and contributed services, but concludes that charter schools' funding—and thus their opportunities to serve children effectively—are arbitrarily limited by state law and policy.

In chapter 3, Paul E. Peterson, Nat Torinus, and Brad Smith consider the effects of local conditions on the emergence of new charter schools and other schools of choice. They spotlight Milwaukee, where circumstances are especially positive for charters. Based on the Milwaukee experience they conclude, like Hoxby, that the supply of schools of choice is highly elastic. The number and quality of schools of choice depend on official policy and community politics. A locality that sets moderate barriers to entry and creates a stable funding and operating environment for schools is likely to experience rapid growth of new schools. They argue that quality new schools are most likely to emerge in localites with accountability systems that can close low-performing schools, no matter who runs them.

In chapter 4, Chester E. Finn Jr. and Paul T. Hill focus on the problems of public oversight of charter schools. Though every charter school must have a funding and performance agreement with a public agency, the roles of those agencies were poorly thought through, and their activities have often created major barriers to charter school success. The authors suggest how authorizers, still the weakest link in the whole charter school phenomenon, can build capacity for perceptive judgment of school proposals and responsible performance oversight.

In chapter 5, John E. Chubb considers the problem of scale—increasing the number and quality of charter schools so they more fully serve the groups that need them and put school districts under greater competitive pressure. He examines the relative strengths of nonprofit and for-profit organizations for this purpose, and concludes that state laws permitting more open competition between schools run by districts, nonprofits, and for-profits would increase the number of charter schools and improve the overall quality of options available to families.

In chapter 6, Chester E. Finn Jr. assesses the potential for chartering to foster innovation and experimentation. He notes that innovation was one of four goals of the charter movement, and he disagrees with observers who decry the conventionality of charter schools. He lists ten ways in which charters provide innovation in public education. He concludes that even with the challenges charter schools must face, the charter movement has attracted new educational, organizational, and financial talent into public education. Laws and policies establishing a more level playing field for charter schools would stimulate even more fundamental innovation in years to come.

In the final chapter, Paul T. Hill returns to the analysis of state laws and policies established in this introduction, and suggests how conditions more favorable to charter schools can be created. The goal should not be to create a structural advantage for charter schools, but to create a level playing field such that no publicly funded school is handicapped in its effort to educate children. Acknowledging the limits of policy change, he suggests there is a continuing need for philanthropy to help develop resources that charter schools need and school districts won't or can't provide. But nothing else matters as much as policy change, which must be achieved in the face of political forces that caused the playing field to be tilted against charter schools in the first place. The final chapter sets priorities for policy changes and suggests how charter supporters can organize to make them happen.

1. The Supply of Charter Schools

Caroline M. Hoxby

Over the past decade, the numbers of charter schools and charter school students have grown rapidly in the U.S. In the 2005–06 school year, 3,625 charter schools were in operation. Yet, just thirteen years earlier, in the 1992–93 school year, just a single charter school operated. In 2003–04, which is the most recent school year for which we have reliable enrollment statistics, charter schools served 789,025 students, up from the mere handful with which the lone school had started eleven years earlier. In spite of all this growth, however, charter schools served only 1.6 percent of American public school students in the 2003–04 school year.

Thus, when someone asks whether charter schools are important, a reasonable person looking at the statistics might not know what to say. In fact, the answer depends on whether the supply of charter schools is *elastic*. That is, will the supply of places in charter schools expand so long as there is demand for them? Or, is the supply of places that currently exists just about all we will ever see? Some commentators have speculated that we will simply run out of suitable buildings for charter schools or, more importantly, run out of people who are interested in teaching in them. Such speculations embody the idea that charter schools are not an elastic part of normal American schooling, but peculiar institutions that exist as experiments only.

If the supply of places is elastic, then charter schools may well be an important part of the future of American education—a relevant schooling option for many families and a force with which regular public schools will have to reckon. If the supply is inelastic, then charter schools may end up being just another special case that warrants explanatory footnotes. Today, we tend to treat homeschooling and alternative schools for dropout-prone youth as special cases.

This study investigates whether the supply of charter schools is elastic and what factors promote greater supply. It turns out that differences in states' charter school laws are the primary reason why the supply of places for students in charter schools differs across areas of the U.S. If a state's law simultaneously allows charter schools and creates an environment that is hostile to them, few places for students are created in charter schools. In contrast, the supply of charter school places is much greater in states whose laws create an even playing field between charter schools and regular public schools. The evidence presented in this study suggests that the key elements of an even playing field are funding that is commensurate with that of the local regular public schools, fiscal autonomy, and operational autonomy at start-up. The evidence also indicates that teachers' unions create an environment that is hostile to charter schools. At one level, these findings should hardly come as a surprise. At another level, proponents of charter schools have often been forced into political compromises wherein they see a law enacted that provides charter schools with highly unequal funding and little autonomy. The results presented in this study suggest that they may be "giving up the baby with the bath water."

Any study of supply must account properly for the factors that influence *demand*. This is because the number of charter school places we observe is the result of the interaction between supply and demand. Thus, as a bonus of sorts, this study presents evidence on the factors that raise demand for charter schools. Simple economics would lead us to expect that there will be more demand for charter schools in areas where there are families who do not otherwise get to exercise choice, either because one or only a few public school districts monopolize the local "market" or because they are too disadvantaged to exercise choice. The latter case might exist, for example, where there is ample choice among public school districts only for families who are able to buy a house in the suburbs.

What One Needs to Know about Charter School Growth

Minnesota was the first state to pass a charter school law, in 1991, and by the 1992–93 school year, its one charter school was the pioneer for the nation. Thereafter, other states enacted charter school laws: California in 1992; Colorado, Georgia, Massachusetts, Michigan, New Mexico, and Wisconsin in 1993; and so on. The entire range of legal enactment dates is shown in Table 1.1. Within two years of enactment, the typical state began seeing some charter schools open their doors to students and thereafter saw relatively steady growth. We can see by examining Figure 1.1, which shows that, once begun, the growth in the number of charter schools in the U.S. proceeded at a very steady rate. Indeed, the line is nearly straight from 1997 to 2005, indicating a stable rate of growth.

Nevertheless, the growth in charter schools was by no means the same in every state that enacted a law. Mississippi's law was passed in 1997, yet the state still had only a single charter school

Table 1.1 Number of Charter Schools in Operation by School Year

State	*Year of Charter Law*	*1992–93*	*1993–94*	*1994–95*	*1995–96*	*1996–97*	*1997–98*	*1998–99*	*1999–00*	*2000–01*	*2001–02*	*2002–03*	*2003–04*	*2004–05*	*2005–06*	*Percent of All Schools*
Alabama																0.0%
Alaska	1995	0	0	0	1	1	8	11	12	13	13	14	17	20	24	4.5%
Arizona	1994	0	1	2	36	85	125	167	225	292	353	407	429	442	449	21.4%
Arkansas	1995	0	0	0	0	0	0	0	0	0	3	6	11	16	17	1.5%
California	1992	0	22	47	68	89	102	127	193	250	308	366	432	511	592	6.3%
Colorado	1993	0	3	12	21	29	50	58	65	76	85	91	97	105	116	6.7%
Connecticut	1996	0	0	0	0	0	8	9	11	11	11	12	12	15	15	1.2%
Delaware	1995	0	0	0	0	2	3	5	5	9	11	13	15	15	15	7.2%
D.C.	1996	0	0	0	0	1	2	13	24	30	34	37	39	49	65	31.3%
Florida	1996	0	0	0	0	4	27	56	88	121	162	191	219	272	326	9.0%
Georgia	1993	0	0	0	2	3	4	8	10	15	20	28	33	37	49	2.0%
Hawaii	1994	0	0	0	1	2	2	2	2	9	22	25	26	27	27	9.5%
Idaho	1998	0	0	0	0	0	0	1	4	4	5	11	14	17	23	3.3%
Illinois	1996	0	0	0	0	0	5	13	17	18	22	25	29	33	41	0.9%
Indiana	2001	0	0	0	0	0	0	0	0	0	0	11	15	22	29	1.4%
Iowa	2002	0	0	0	0	0	0	0	0	0	0	0	0	3	7	0.5%
Kansas	1994	0	0	0	0	0	0	6	6	7	16	17	19	28	33	2.3%
Kentucky																0.0%
Louisiana	1995	0	0	0	0	2	5	8	10	13	15	16	16	17	21	1.3%
Maine																0.0%
Maryland	2003	0	0	0	0	0	0	0	0	0	0	0	0	1	15	1.1%
Massachusetts	1993	0	0	0	14	20	21	30	36	38	40	45	48	54	57	2.9%
Michigan	1993	0	0	4	41	73	99	132	168	180	189	195	206	226	233	5.6%
Minnesota	1991	1	5	10	13	15	20	31	46	57	67	76	86	103	126	4.8%
Mississippi	1997	0	0	0	0	0	0	1	1	1	1	1	1	1	1	0.1%

Missouri	1998	0	0	0	0	0	0	0	14	19	20	25	26	26	26	1.1%
Montana																0.0%
Nebraska																0.0%
Nevada	1997	0	0	1	1	1	1	1	5	6	8	11	14	20	20	3.5%
New Hampshire	1995	0	0	0	0	0	0	0	0	0	0	0	0	2	6	1.6%
New Jersey	1996	0	0	0	0	0	12	26	35	39	43	45	47	49	52	1.3%
New Mexico	1993	0	0	1	1	1	1	1	2	10	21	27	34	42	51	5.8%
New York	1998	0	0	0	0	0	0	0	2	14	27	34	46	58	79	2.1%
North Carolina	1996	0	0	0	0	0	26	47	62	77	85	91	93	97	100	4.4%
North Dakota																0.0%
Ohio	1997	0	0	0	0	0	0	14	39	60	90	130	162	240	277	6.5%
Oklahoma	1999	0	0	0	0	0	0	0	1	6	10	10	13	13	13	0.7%
Oregon	1999	0	0	0	0	0	0	0	1	7	13	20	36	50	62	4.7%
Pennsylvania	1997	0	0	0	0	0	7	26	44	62	72	85	95	104	115	3.5%
Rhode Island	1995	0	0	0	0	0	1	2	2	3	6	9	10	11	11	3.2%
South Carolina	1996	0	0	0	0	0	0	1	5	6	7	10	15	20	26	0.0%
South Dakota																2.2%
Tennessee	2002	0	0	0	0	0	0	0	0	0	0	0	4	7	12	0.7%
Texas	1995	0	0	0	0	15	20	101	156	176	208	224	233	251	259	3.1%
Utah	1998	0	0	0	0	0	0	3	5	7	7	10	17	28	39	4.3%
Vermont																0.0%
Virginia	1998	0	0	0	0	0	0	0	0	0	3	5	5	5	5	0.2%
Washington																0.0%
West Virginia																0.0%
Wisconsin	1993	0	0	1	8	12	17	28	45	74	92	112	129	162	188	8.2%
Wyoming	1995	0	0	0	0	0	0	0	0	0	0	1	1	2	3	0.8%
Nation		1	31	78	207	355	566	928	1341	1710	2089	2436	2744	3201	3625	

Notes: This table is based on Center for Education Reform (2005). It shows the number of charter schools that are still in operation, by the year in which they open, cumulatively.

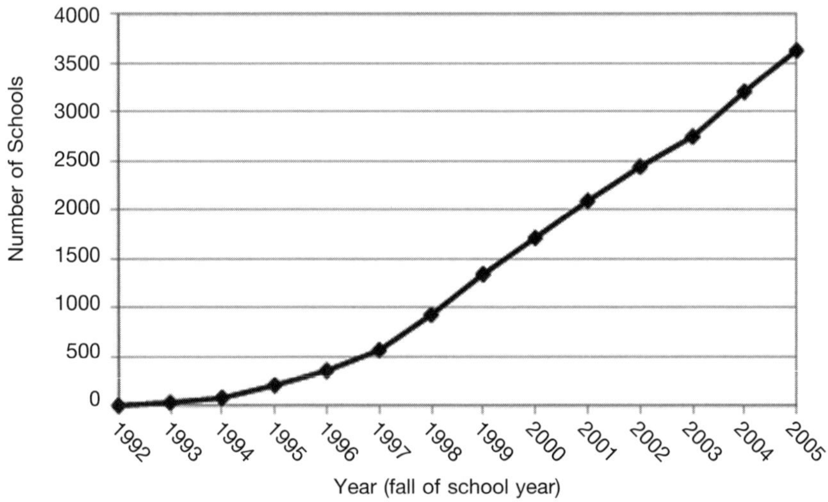

Fig. 1.1 Number of Charter Schools in the United States

operating eight years later. At the other end of the spectrum, Arizona enacted a law in 1994 and had 407 schools operating eight years later. These and the numbers for all other states are shown in Table 1.1. As of the 2005–06 school year, the states with the largest share of their public schools set up as charter schools were Arizona (21.4 percent), Hawaii (9.5 percent), Florida (9.0 percent), and Wisconsin (8.2 percent). The District of Columbia is something of a special case because it contains a city with no suburbs or rural areas: 31.3 percent of its schools are charter schools.

As shown in Figure 1.2, national charter school enrollment also grew at a very steady pace from 1997 onwards. The line shown on the figure is nearly straight, indicating stable growth. (The 1997–98 school year is the first for which we have reasonably reliable charter school enrollment data. Before that time, states were inconsistent about classifying schools as charter schools.) The growth in enrollment was by no means similar in

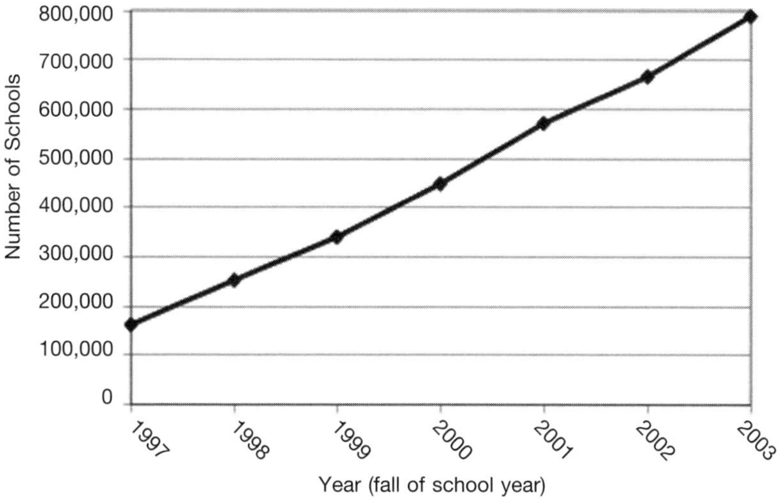

Fig. 1.2 Charter School Students in the United States

each state, however. Table 1.2 shows that Kansas, for instance, passed a charter school law in 1994 and yet had only 0.3 percent of its students enrolled in charter schools in the 2003–04 school year. Arizona also passed its law in 1994 but had 8.0 percent of its students in charter schools by 2003–04. In the District of Columbia, 16.6 percent of students attend charter schools. All states' enrollment histories are shown in Table 1.2.

The steady national growth rates in the number of charter schools and charter school students disguise very substantial variation in growth rates among states. It could be differences in *demand* that explains all this variation. Perhaps people in Mississippi and Kansas simply do not want to attend charter schools, regardless of how available they are. Perhaps people in Arizona, Hawaii, Florida, Wisconsin, and the District of Columbia are simply very eager to attend charter schools and will overcome obstacles to do so. Differences in the environment for *supply* could also, however, explain the variation in growth rates. The

Table 1.2 Charter School Enrollment, by School Year

	Year of Law	*1997–98*	*1998–99*	*1999–00*	*2000–01*	*2001–02*	*2002–03*	*2003–04*	*Percent of All Students*
Alabama									0.0%
Alaska	1995	1,097	2,126	2,300	2,594	2,327	2,577	3,476	2.6%
Arizona	1994	25,128	32,209	31,176	45,596	61,571	56,632	81,723	8.0%
Arkansas	1995				708	1,083		2,719	0.6%
California	1992	55,764	73,905	104,730	115,582	132,807	156,696	166,204	2.6%
Colorado	1993	10,888	13,911	17,822	20,155	24,658	28,785	31,529	4.2%
Connecticut	1996	1,084	1,875	2,148	2,429	2,594	2,198	2,222	0.4%
Delaware	1995	365	992		2,716	4,230	5,060	6,241	5.3%
D.C.	1996	235	3,364	6,432		6,943	8,644	12,958	16.6%
Florida	1996	3,123	10,561	17,251	26,893	40,468	51,698	67,466	2.6%
Georgia	1993	14,522	18,611	11,005	20,066	24,656	25,732	26,752	1.8%
Hawaii	1994	832	841	790	1,343	3,071	3,354	4,502	2.5%
Idaho	1998		57	915	1,083	1,478	3,056	4,811	1.9%
Illinois	1996	2,117	3,379	6,152	7,552	8,661	7,464	11,740	0.6%
Indiana	2001						1,271	2,906	0.3%
Iowa									0.0%
Kansas	1994	70	1,545			1,465	1,944	1,389	0.3%
Kentucky									0.0%
Louisiana	1995	463	1,589	2,449	3,212	3,923	4,730	4,585	0.6%
Maine									0.0%
Maryland	2003							196	0.0%
Massachusetts	1993	6,360	9,673	12,518	13,712	14,446	15,912	17,971	1.8%
Michigan	1993	18,273	25,294	46,078	54,751	64,598	68,072	72,096	4.1%
Minnesota	1991	2,892	4,670	7,794	9,395	10,206	12,144	14,210	1.7%
Mississippi	1997		340	347	367	351	335	338	0.1%

Missouri	1998			4,303	7,061	7,694	9,743	10,304	1.1%
Montana									0.0%
Nebraska									0.0%
Nevada	1997			898	1,255	1,945	2,788	3,917	1.0%
New Hampshire									1.9%
New Jersey	1996	1,424	4,001		10,179	11,706	12,526	12,804	0.9%
New Mexico	1993	4,563	4,601		1,335	2,697	4,404	6,225	0.5%
New York	1998						10,396	14,572	0.0%
North Carolina	1996	4,488	9,513	12,691	15,523	18,235	20,420	21,955	1.6%
North Dakota									0.0%
Ohio	1997		2,509	9,809	14,745	22,569	33,828	45,838	2.5%
Oklahoma	1999				1,208	2,133	2,712	3,491	0.6%
Oregon	1999			109	559	999	1,959	2,487	0.5%
Pennsylvania	1997	974	5,474	11,413	18,981	28,453	32,860	41,114	2.3%
Rhode Island	1995	190	397	446	557	843	705	1,024	0.7%
South Carolina	1996	156	364	327	484	459	1,132	3,153	0.0%
South Dakota									0.0%
Tennessee	2002							324	0.0%
Texas	1995	5,533	18,590	25,687	37,978	47,050	53,984	60,833	1.4%
Utah	1998			390	537	656	1,552	3,239	0.7%
Vermont									0.0%
Virginia	1998				55	813	464	476	0.0%
Washington									0.0%
West Virginia									0.0%
Wisconsin	1993	1,589	2,060	3,561	9,511	15,241	18,998	21,113	2.4%
Wyoming	1995						102	132	0.2%

Notes: Enrollment data for charter schools is systematically understated and not always available for a state that has operating schools. This is due to states' not reporting schools' charter status in a systematic way. The problem particularly affects early years such as 1997–98 and 1998–99. Missing data does not necessarily mean that enrollment was zero, especially if Table 1 indicates that the state had operational charter schools. The sources are author's calculations based on U.S. Department of Education (1999, 2000) and on the Common Core of Data, 1998–99 through 2003–04 school years.

environment for charter schools in each state is determined by the details of its law.

A Brief Survey of States' Legal Environments

The environment that each state creates for its charter schools is a function of the law that governs their start-up, operation, and continuance. Most analysts of charter school laws look at a variety of indicators but have one simple question in mind: is the state putting the charter schools on an even playing field or is it crippling their ability to thrive, no matter how good an education they provide? Several sub-questions are crucial. Do charter schools have sufficient funding? Is their funding at all commensurate with that of regular local public schools? The answers to these questions matter because, regardless of how efficient and economical they are, charter schools must hire teachers in competition with regular public schools, they must lease or buy space in a competitive real estate market, and they must pay utility bills and the like. It may be particularly hard for a charter school to succeed if teachers must take a substantial pay cut to work in it. In addition, charter schools face the same safety, health, facilities, and accountability standards that other public schools face, so it is hard for them to provide, say, the same square feet per student if they have only a small fraction of the budget to spend on a physical plant.

Another important sub-question is whether a charter school is fiscally autonomous. It is easiest to understand the importance of fiscal autonomy by considering the concrete example of a charter school that is succeeding in attracting great numbers of applicants who are drawn from the local public school district. If the charter school is fiscally autonomous, it may be able to continue growing so long as it can expand its operation on whatever its set per-pupil revenue is. If the school is not autonomous, however, its budget is held by its local district and it must negotiate for the budget's release. A charter school that is "too" successful may find itself in a tense conference with officials from the local district, who may decide that they need to reduce the charter school's per-pupil revenue. The officials may even tell the school that its success is evidence that it is getting too much revenue per pupil. Clearly, a lack of fiscal autonomy can set off a negative spiral in which success is punished by financial deprivation. In such circumstances, charter schools may hesitate to expand for fear of attracting attention and triggering financial austerity.

Operational autonomy is important as well. While all charter schools are held accountable for their achievement and certain outcomes, through their states' accountability systems and the federal No Child Left Behind act, not all charter schools have equal ability to set their own curriculum, salaries, benefit schedule, disciplinary standard, and other matters of management. The first time that operational autonomy is an issue is at the school's start-up. If it lacks autonomy then, it may be forced to accept operational methods that undermine its ability to succeed. For instance, in some states, a charter school needs to prove that it has local support for its start-up (not merely prove that it can attract students and satisfy state standards). The approval of the local district is often crucial, in practice, in demonstrating local support. Yet, the local district may condition its approval on the charter school's not growing beyond a certain size, accepting space in an unsuitable building, being strictly oriented toward at-risk or dropout-prone students, participating in most or all of the local district's purchasing and salary contracts, and so on. Once the charter school has started up, continuing operational autonomy may be an issue.

Although a variety of authors and organizations have surveyed states' charter school laws, the analyses that are the most detailed and consistent over time have been carried out by experts convened by the Center for Education Reform (2003, 2004) and the Fordham Foundation (Palmer and Gau, 2003). This study employs the Center for Education Reform's ratings simply because they cover the most states. They are also easily interpretable and widely known. It is important for a study of this type *not* to construct its own ratings. It is desirable to have an arms-length relationship between the researchers who rate laws that serve as potential explanatory factors and the researcher who evaluates the effects of laws on the supply of charter schools.

For the analysis that follows, which focuses on the most recent enrollment data available (for the 2003–04 school year), the 2003 ratings are the most appropriate ones. Consequently, Table 1.3 shows the Center for Education Reform's 2003 ratings of states' charter school laws. A score of five on an aspect of the law means that the state puts the charter schools on an even playing field on this particular dimension. A score of zero means that the state puts the charter schools at a great disadvantage, relative to the regular public schools, on this particular dimension. All aspects of the law listed in the table are defined with some precision in the notes below the table. The definitions are from the Center for Education Reform. The variables that correspond most closely to the issues of funding and autonomy already discussed are listed toward the left-hand side of the table.

Consider fiscal autonomy. Arizona, Delaware, Florida, Indiana, Massachusetts, Michigan, Minnesota, and New Jersey all receive scores of five, indicating that their charter schools' budgets cannot be held hostage by their local districts. In Arkansas, Iowa, Kansas, Maryland, Mississippi, New Hampshire, and Virginia, the law gets a rating of zero because a local district can hold up a charter school's budget with relative ease.

Consider whether charter schools are guaranteed full or relatively full per pupil funding. The District of Columbia, Florida, Massachusetts, Michigan, and North Carolina all get scores of four and a half or above. Their charter schools can afford salaries and supplies similar to those of regular public schools—though some caution is necessary here because charter schools are often left out of state mechanisms that subsidize the purchase or lease of buildings and other capital. Iowa, Kansas, Mississippi, New Hampshire, Utah, and Virginia all get scores *below* one, which suggests that their charter schools are severely revenue-deprived compared to the regular public schools with which they compete.

Readers can examine the remaining columns of the table for themselves. It is important to note that the ratings of various aspects of a state's law tends to be correlated with one another. In other words, states that give charter schools fiscal autonomy also tend to give them fuller funding, more operational autonomy, exemptions from local collective bargaining agreements, more ability to expand, and so on. This correlation poses something of a problem: it will prove hard to tell whether it is really fiscal autonomy or, say, exemptions from local collective bargaining agreements that matter if the two aspects of the law tend to be both favorable or both unfavorable. In fact, in the analysis that follows, it is not possible to assign separate credit to each of the ten aspects of the laws recorded by the Center for Education Reform. Instead, the analysis focuses on just the first four aspects listed—this is the maximum that can be used while maintaining reasonably straightforward interpretation.

Some Pointers on the Analysis that Follows

The data used in the analysis below include the Center for Education Reform's ratings, shown in Table 1.3; the number of charter schools and charter school students in 2003–04, summarized in Tables 1.1 and 1.2 derived from the Common Core of Data (U.S. Department of Education, 1999 through 2005), two U.S. Department of Education Reports (1999, 2000), and Center for

Table 1.3 Environment for Charter Schools, by State

State	Fiscal Autonomy	Autonomy at Start-Up	Continuing Legal/ Operational Autonomy	Guaranteed Full Per-Pupil Funding	Number of Schools Allowed	New Starts Allowed	Multiple Chartering Authorities	Variety of Applicants	Automatic Waiver from State Rules	Exempt from Local Collective Bargain
Alaska	1	1	0	3.5	2.3	5	1	5	0	0
Arizona	5	5	5	3.5	4.5	4.75	4	5	4.5	4.75
Arkansas	0	2.5	2	1.5	2	4.5	2.5	2	0	0
California	3	3	2	3	5	4.75	4	5	2	4
Colorado	4.5	3	2.75	4	4.5	4.5	3	5	3.25	4.5
Connecticut	3	1	0.5	3.5	1.5	4.5	2.5	1.5	2.5	2.5
Delaware	5	3.5	4	5	5	4.5	4	5	3.5	5
D.C.	4.5	3	4.5	4.5	4.5	4.75	4	5	5	5
Florida	5	3	3.5	5	4	4.5	1.75	5	3	4.5
Georgia	2	2.5	1	2	5	4.5	1.5	5	0	1.5
Hawaii	1	2	0.5	1.5	2	4.5	1	3	4.5	0
Idaho	1	1	0	3	2.6	4.5	1.3	5	4.3	1
Illinois	3.5	1	2	3	1.75	4.5	1.75	4	3	2.5
Indiana	5	3	3	3	4	4.75	4.5	4	5	3
Iowa	0	1.5	0	0	1	0	1	0	3	0
Kansas	0	1	0	0.5	1	4.5	1	0	0.5	0
Louisiana	4.5	2	1	3	2	4.5	1.75	3.5	2.5	1.5
Maryland	0	1	0	2	1	4	1.5	2	0	0
Massachusetts	5	4	4.7	5	3.3	4.5	3.5	4.3	3	3
Michigan	5	5	5	5	4.5	4.75	4.5	5	2.7	3
Minnesota	5	3.5	4.5	3.5	5	4.75	4.5	5	5	4.5
Mississippi	0	0	0	0	0	0	1	0	1.3	0
Missouri	4	4	3.5	4	2	3	3.5	4	4	4
Nevada	1	5	1.5	3.5	2	4.5	1	2	2.5	0
New Hampshire	0	3	2	0	5	2	4	3	4	5
New Jersey	5	3	2	2	5	4.5	3	4	1	3
New Mexico	2	3	2.75	3	3.5	4.5	1.75	5	2	2.5
New York	4	4	5	2.5	2.3	4.5	4	4	5	3

North Carolina	4	3	3	4.5	3	4.75	3	5	4	3
Ohio	3	5	3	3.5	3	4.5	4.5	5	3	3
Oklahoma	3	5	1	2	2	4.5	1	4	2.5	4
Oregon	2.5	5	3	2.5	5	3.5	1.5	5	2.5	4.25
Pennsylvania	3.5	3.5	3	3	5	4.5	1.75	5	3	4.5
Rhode Island	1.5	0	0.5	3.5	1	4.5	1	2.54	0.5	0
South Carolina	2	2	2	2	5	4.5	1.75	4	2.5	3
Tennessee	1	2	0	3	2	4	1.75	4	0	3
Texas	3	3.5	2	3	3	4.75	3.25	4.25	0	4
Utah	1	2.5	1.6	0.3	1.5	4.5	3	4	0.6	4
Virginia	0	2.5	0.5	0.5	1.6	4.5	1	4.5	0.5	0
Wisconsin	1.8	2.5	2.5	2	5	4.75	3.5	5	2.5	2.5
Wyoming	1	2.5	0	1.5	5	4.5	1.75	5	0.5	0

Notes: The table is borrowed from Center for Education Review (2003). It shows states' support for autonomous charter schools, as indicated by their laws, which were rated as of December 2002 by the Center for Education Reform. States not shown had no charter school law on their books in December 2002.

Fiscal Autonomy: States that give charter schools full control over their own budgets, without the district holding the funds, encourage more activity than states that do not.

Autonomy at start-up (formal evidence of local support): States that permit charter schools to be formed without having to prove specified levels of local support encourage more activity than states that require such demonstrations of support.

Continuing legal/operational autonomy: States in which charter schools are independent legal entities that can own property, sue and be sued, incur debt, control budget and personnel, and contract for services encourage more activity than states in which charter schools remain under district jurisdiction. In addition, legal autonomy refers to the ability of charter schools to control enrollment numbers, with no special conditions imposed by the charter law or the local district on its policies.

Guaranteed full funding: States where 100% of per-pupil funding automatically follows student enrolled in charter schools encourage more activity than states where the amount of funding is automatically set below 100%, or must be negotiated with the district.

Number of Schools: States that permit an unlimited or substantial number of autonomous charter schools encourage more activity than states that either limit the number of autonomous schools, or allow an unlimited number of charter schools with restrictions on their autonomy, demographics, etc.

New starts: States that permit new schools to start up encourage more activity than those that permit only public school conversions.

Multiple chartering authorities: States that permit a number of entities in addition to or instead of local school boards to authorize charter schools encourage more activity than those that vest authorizing power in a single entity, particularly if that entity is the local school board, or provide an appeals process.

Variety of applicants: States that permit a variety of individuals and groups both inside and outside the existing public school system to start charter schools encourage more activity than states that limit eligible applicants to public schools or public school personnel.

Automatic waiver from laws and regulations: States that provide automatic blanket waivers from most or all state and district education laws, regulations, and policies encourage more activity than states that provide no waivers or require charter schools to negotiate waivers on an issue-by-issue basis with charter-granting authorities. (In no case, however, are civil rights laws or health/safety codes waived for charter schools.)

Exemption from collective bargaining agreements / district work rules: States that give charter schools complete control over personnel decisions encourage more activity than states where charter school teachers must remain subject to the terms of district collective bargaining agreements or work rules.

Education Reform reports (2003, 2004, 2005). In addition, the data include characteristics of each county in the U.S., derived from U.S. Department of Education (2003). The characteristics selected are those that are likely to affect the demand for charter schools, and they are further described in the Data Appendix.

In the analysis that follows, a regression is used to show how supply and demand factors explain the variation among counties in the number of their students who are enrolled in charter schools. Regression is a statistical technique that separates the variation in an outcome—in this case, the number of students in charter schools—into parts associated with the variation in multiple explanatory factors. Another regression is used to show how the same factors explain the variation among counties in the number of charter schools operating.

The analysis is conducted at the county level because, within a state, counties differ greatly in their characteristics, especially the conditions likely to affect demand for charter schools. For instance, only one county might offer families a lot of school choice within the regular public sector. Another county might offer them none. Readers who are interested in statistical details may wish to know that the standard errors are robust and clustered at the level of the state, owing to the fact that charter school laws vary only at that level.

Explaining the Number of Students Enrolled in Charter Schools

Table 1.4 shows the main results of this study. The factors that affect the number of charter school students in a county are divided into those that mainly affect the supply of charter schools, those that mainly affect the demand for charter schools, and those that affect both supply and demand. The division into these groups is only approximate. Aspects of the state's charter school

Table 1.4 Determinants of the Number of Charter School Students
Dependent Variable: ln(Number of Charter School Students in a County)

	Main Results	Including Teachers' Unionization
Factors that Mainly Affect Charter School Supply		
ln(Charter School Revenue Per Pupil, in thousands)	**0.42**	**0.38**
Years Since Charter Law Passed	**0.58**	**0.75**
Fiscal Autonomy (1–5 scale)	**0.81**	**1.80**
Autonomy at Start-Up (1–5 Scale)	0.41	−0.10
Legal/Operational Autonomy (1–5 scale)	**−1.30**	**−1.39**
Guaranteed Full Per-Pupil Funding (1–5 scale)	**0.22**	0.02
Share of Teachers Who Are Union Members (0–1 scale)		**−1.13**
Factors that Mainly Affect the Demand for Charter Schools		
ln(black students in county)	**0.40**	**0.53**
ln(Hispanic and other race students in county)	**−0.25**	**−0.26**
ln(White students in county)	**0.57**	**0.58**
ln(Asian students in county)	**−0.19**	**−0.14**
ln(households with income less than $30,000)	0.44	0.39
ln(magnet school students in county)	−0.04	−0.07
Index of Choice among Public School Districts (0–1 scale)	**−1.08**	**−1.44**
ln(special education students in county)	0.39	0.43
ln(English language learners in county)	**0.09**	**0.06**
Factors that Affect Both Supply and Demand		
large city	−0.01	−0.01
mid-sized city	−0.01	**−0.05**
urban fringe of a large city	**−0.30**	**−0.33**
urban fringe of a mid-sized city	**−0.32**	**−0.34**
large town	**−0.12**	**−0.14**
small town	**−0.09**	**−0.10**
rural but inside metropolitan statistical area	**−0.06**	**−0.11**
rural and outside metropolitan statistical area	0.08	0.05
constant	**−11.63**	**−13.70**

Notes: The table shows estimates from linear regressions. Because the dependent variable is in natural log units, one may interpret the coefficient as the *percentage change effect* of the explanatory variable. If the explanatory variable is also in natural log units, then one may interpret the coefficient as the percentage change effect of a percentage change effect in the explanatory variable. For instance, the first coefficient shown indicates that if there a 100 percent change in the per-pupil revenue of charter schools, the number of charter school students would rise by 0.42 or 42 percent. To take another example, with each year after the passage of a charter school law, enrollment grows by 0.58 or 58 percent. (Remember that charter school enrollment usually starts from a *tiny* base.) A coefficient that is shown in bold typeface is statistically significantly different from zero at the 0.15 level. The standard errors were computed to be robust with clustering at the level of the state. The variables that are measured on a scale of 1 to 5 are such that a higher value corresponds to more of the property in question—for instance, more fiscal autonomy. See Table 1.3 and data appendix for details on variables.

law are listed under supply factors because they influence how feasible and attractive it is to run a charter school, given the potential population of students. Socio-demographic variables that describe local students are listed under demand factors because they describe the potential demanders of charter schools. If, for instance, English language learners demand charter schools more or less than other students, the socio-demographic variables will allow us to account for it. Finally, the series of indicator variables for different levels of urbanicity are supply factors because it is harder to run a charter school in an area with dispersed population than one with a dense population. This is simply because, unlike a regular public school that serves a compact geographic "attendance area," a charter school must typically gather its students from across a few attendance areas. The more rural the charter school, the more mired it will be in transportation difficulties. The indicators for urbanicity are also related to supply because the cultural background, employment, and education of parents who live in cities may make them more or less interested in demanding charter schools.

The first thing to note about Table 1.4 is that most of the factors listed have a statistically significant effect on the number of students enrolled in charter schools. (Coefficients shown in bold are statistically significantly different from zero at the 15 percent level, and the vast majority of these are statistically significant at the 5 percent level.) This tells us immediately that the supply of charter schools *is* elastic. If they were not elastically supplied, there would be little variation in the number of students in charter schools generated by variables in either supply or demand factors and, as a result, the factors would tend not to have a statistically significant effect.

Second, the supply factors have sizable effects on charter school enrollment. Because the dependent variable is in natural log units, one may interpret the coefficient as the percentage change effect of the explanatory variable. If the explanatory variable is also in natural log units, then one may interpret the coefficient as the percentage change effect of a percentage change effect in the explanatory variable. Remember that charter school enrollment usually starts from a tiny base so that large percentage changes may correspond to a smaller number of students than one might suppose at a glance. The first coefficient shown indicates that if there is a 100 percent change in the per-pupil revenue of charter schools, the number of charter school students would rise by 0.42 or 42 percent. The second coefficient shows that with each year after the passage of a charter school law, charter school enrollment grows by an average of 0.58 or 58 percent. Each point on the fiscal autonomy scale raises the number of charter school students by 81 percent; a point of initial operating autonomy has an insignificant effect (but a positive coefficient); and a point on the guaranteed full funding scale raises the number of charter school students by 22 percent. Greater continuing operating autonomy has, however, a *negative* effect on charter school enrollment. This result will be left as somewhat puzzling for now, but it will be explained below.

The right-hand column of Table 1.4 shows what happens to the coefficients on the supply factors if we introduce a measure of teacher unionism—specifically, the share of teachers in the county who are union members. This variable has a large negative effect: if the share unionized rises by 0.10 (10 percent), then charter school enrollment drops by 11.3 percent. Also, the inclusion of the unionization variable makes the effect of full funding drop to zero. The way to interpret this evidence is that a powerful union presence creates an environment in which charter schools do not get funding that is commensurate with that of regular public schools. Thus, unions may have a direct effect on the supply of charter schools—perhaps by creating a hostile climate—

but they also have an indirect effect through their influence on the law that gets enacted.

The bottom part of the table shows us the effect of demand factors. For convenience, focus on the column without the unionization variable. The most interesting coefficient is effect of choice among public school districts. If the choice index rises by 0.25, which corresponds to a shift from two to four districts in the county, then charter school enrollment falls by 27 percent (108 × 0.25). Magnet school enrollment has a small and negative coefficient that is statistically insignificant. This evidence suggests that magnet schools are not an alternative form of choice that parents consider to be equivalent to charter schools, probably because magnet schools have very little autonomy from their parent districts (relative either to another district or a charter school). Put another way, families appear to have a demand simply for exercising meaningful choice over schools—that is, choice over schools that are sufficiently autonomous to differ. When families can exercise choice easily within the regular public school sector, they are less inclined to charter schools.

Black and white students are about equally likely to demand charter schools, but Asian students are less likely to demand them. The coefficients on Hispanic and English language learners may be interpreted together because the vast majority of English language learners are native Spanish speakers. Interpreted together, they suggest that Hispanics whose first language is not English are more likely to demand charter schools, but that Hispanics who are native English speakers are less likely to demand charter schools. In other words, students who classified themselves as Hispanics vary a lot, from recent immigrants to people whose ancestors immigrated generations ago. It is recent immigrants among the Hispanics who demand charter schools more. There is a large and positive but statistically insignificant coefficient for students whose families have less than \$30,000 in income. While we cannot conclude that poor students are more likely to demand charter schools, they do not appear less likely to do so either. (In fact, the coefficient is just on the border of being significant so we can rule out poor students demanding charter schools substantially less than others.) On the whole, the socio-demographic coefficients suggest that disadvantaged students are more likely to demand charter schools. This is not surprising, both because it accords with other evidence on who attends charter schools and because it is sensible. Advantaged families usually have numerous school choices in the regular public and private school sectors, so they are less likely to rely on charter schools in order to exercise choice.

Finally, the coefficients on the indicators for urbanicity suggest that we are most likely to find charter schools in densely populated central cities of urban areas or in rural areas. We are least likely to find them in the suburbs of major cities. This makes sense. A large district often monopolizes the central city of a metropolitan area, giving central city students little choice. Also, it should be more feasible to run a charter school in a central city area (apart from problems associated with buildings). Rural families also tend to lack school choice, especially if they live in a vast consolidated district. While running a charter school in a rural area may create transportation difficulties, some rural charter schools are small enough to serve a "pocket" of families who do not want their children to travel to a district consolidated school. Also rural charter schools have been pioneers in making use of the Internet to overcome transportation difficulties.

Which Charter Schools Are Most Elastic?

The Appendix Table presents results that show how the supply and demand factors affect charter school enrollment among various subgroups of students. From its results, we can take away a few key findings. First, charter school places in the elementary and middle school grades appear to be more elastic than those in the high school grades. That is, if a state changes its law so it provides more of an even playing field for charter schools, it can expect enrollment to increase more in the elementary and middle than in the high school grades. Second, commensurate per-pupil funding is important for increasing the supply of places in charter schools that will attract enrollment by white students (more important than it is for black or Hispanic students). This may be because white students have regular public school options that are relatively attractive so their families are unwilling to see their child in a school that appears to be pinched for pennies. Black and Hispanic students may see their regular public school options as less attractive, even if they have many resources in theory. This might be the case because black and Hispanic students disproportionately attend run-down or chaotic schools located in districts with high per-pupil spending. Third, fiscal autonomy is important for increasing the supply of places in charter schools that will attract enrollment by black or Hispanic students (more important than it is for white students). One suspects that this is because black and Hispanic students are more likely to reside in politicized regular public school districts where tension over a charter school's being "too" successful might actually end in its budget being held up. Finally, higher per-pupil funding and commensurate per-pupil funding are important for ensuring that there is a supply of charter schools to students who are eligible for free or reduced-price lunch (that is, within 185 percent of the federal poverty line). Perhaps because poor children can bring few resources to school from theirs homes, it is harder to run a charter school on a shoestring if the students being served are poor. Their families are less able to compensate for materials that the school lacks.

Explaining the Number of Charter Schools

Table 1.5 shows results from a regression that attempts to explain the number of charter schools, as opposed to students. Because, for a given number of students, the number of schools will rise if the schools are smaller, this analysis differs from that above mainly in its emphasis on school size.

On the whole, the supply and demand factors that explain charter school enrollment also explain the number of charter schools, in much the same way. There is, however, one exception that is worth noting. Recall that operating autonomy appeared to *decrease* and full funding appeared to increase the supply of charter school places. The evidence in Table 1.5 suggests, in contrast, that operating autonomy increases and full funding decreases the supply of charter *schools*. We can reconcile the results if operating autonomy combined with much-less-than-commensurate funding produces numerous but small charter schools. This is only one possible reconciliation of the results. Others are possible as well.

Summing Up

We have seen that charter schools are elastically supplied. The evidence suggests that greater demand among families is met with a greater number of places. We have also seen that supply is greater in states that have created an environment where charter schools operate on a more even playing field to that of regular public schools. Fiscal autonomy, autonomy at start-up, and commensurate per-pupil funding appear to be the key factors that make a playing field more even, but we should be mindful of the fact that other aspects of state laws may matter a great deal too: we cannot sort out the independent role of some aspects of laws because they are so correlated with the key aspects. If states enact laws that allow charter schools to compete on an equal footing,

Table 1.5 Determinants of the Number of Charter Schools
Dependent Variable: ln(Number of Charter Schools in a County)

Factors that Mainly Affect Charter School Supply	
ln(Charter School Revenue Per Pupil, in thousands)	**0.27**
Years Since Charter Law Passed	**0.28**
Fiscal Autonomy (1–5 scale)	**1.35**
No Need to Prove Local Support (1–5 Scale)	−0.20
Legal/Operational Autonomy (1–5 scale)	**0.78**
Guaranteed Full Per-Pupil Funding (1–5 scale)	**−0.30**
Factors that Mainly Affect the Demand for Charter Schools	
ln(black students in county)	**0.34**
ln(Hispanic students in county)	**−0.17**
ln(White students in county)	**0.37**
ln(Asian students in county)	**−0.18**
ln(households with income less than $30,000)	**0.83**
ln(magnet school students in county)	**−0.06**
Index of Choice among Public School Districts (0–1 scale)	**−0.42**
ln(special education students in county)	0.11
ln(English language learners in county)	**0.11**
Factors that Affect Both Supply and Demand	
large city	−0.01
mid-sized city	**−0.07**
urban fringe of a large city	**−0.29**
urban fringe of a mid-sized city	**−0.28**
large town	**−0.11**
small town	**−0.09**
rural but inside metropolitan statistical area	**−0.24**
rural and outside metropolitan statistical area	**−0.12**
constant	**−11.65**

Notes: The table shows estimates from a linear regression. Because the dependent variable is in natural log units, one may interpret the coefficient as the *percentage change effect* of the explanatory variable. If the explanatory variable is also in natural log units, then one may interpret the coefficient as the percentage change effect of a percentage change effect in the explanatory variable. For instance, the first coefficient shown indicates that if there a 100 percent change in the per-pupil revenue of charter schools, the number of charter schools would rise 0.27 or 27 percent. To take another example, with the average year after the passage of a charter school law, the number of charter schools grows by 0.28 or 28 percent. (Remember that the number of charter schools usually starts from a *tiny* base.) A coefficient that is shown in bold typeface is statistically significantly different from zero at the 0.15 level. The standard errors were computed to be robust with clustering at the level of the state. The variables that are measured on a scale of 1 to 5 are such that a higher value corresponds to more of the property in questionûfor instance, more fiscal autonomy. See Table 1.3 and data appendix for details on variables.

we should expect that they will expand to meet demand. Of course, the "if" is a big "if": we have seen that the local prevalence of teachers' unions reduces charter school supply, in part by generating laws with less commensurate funding. The bottom line is that the details of a charter school law matter. If all laws were like those of the states with the lowest rated laws, charter schools would remain just a marginal phenomenon. If all states' laws were like those rated highest, charter schools might—in another decade or so—be a pervasive and important force in U.S. public education.

Finally, a variety of results suggest that the families who most demand charter schools are those who have little meaningful choice within the regular public school system. In this sense, a law that puts charter schools on an even playing field with regular public schools also puts an important population of *families* on an even playing field with others.

References

Center for Education Reform. *Charter School Laws Across the States: Ranking and Scorecard.* Washington, DC: Center for Education Reform, 2003.

Center for Education Reform. *Charter School Laws Across the States: Ranking and Scorecard.* Washington, DC: Center for Education Reform, 2004.

Center for Education Reform. *Explosive Growth in Charter Schools: A Guide for Charter School Activists.* Washington, DC: Center for Education Reform, 2005.

Palmer, Louann Bierlein, and Rebecca Gau. *Charter School Authorizing: Are States Making the Grade?* Washington, DC: Thomas B. Fordham Institute, 2003.

United States Department of Commerce, Bureau of the Census. *Census of Governments: Employment.* Electronic data. 1987 Census. Washington, DC: Bureau of the Census, 1990.

United States Department of Commerce, Bureau of the Census. *Public Elementary-Secondary Education Finance Data*. Electronic data. Fiscal years 1998 through 2003. Washington, DC: Bureau of the Census, 2000 through 2005.

United States Department of Education, National Center for Education Statistics. *Common Core of Data Public Elementary/Secondary School Universe Survey*. Electronic data. School years 1997–98 through 2003–04. Washington, DC: National Center for Education Statistics, 1999 through 2005.

United States Department of Education, National Center for Education Statistics. *School District Demographics*. Electronic data based on the 2000 United States Census of Population and Housing. Washington, DC: National Center for Education Statistics, 2003.

United States Department of Education, Office of Educational Research and Improvement. *The State of Charter Schools 1999: National Study of Charter Schools*. Third Year Report. Washington, DC: U.S. Department of Education, 1999.

United States Department of Education, Office of Educational Research and Improvement. *The State of Charter Schools 2000: National Study of Charter Schools*. Fourth Year Report. Washington, DC: U.S. Department of Education, 2000.

Appendix

Data on Enrollment and the Number of Schools

The enrollment and number of schools data used in the regression analysis come from the 2003–04 version of the *Common Core of Data* (U.S. Department of Education, 2005). The original data are at the level of the individual school, and they are aggregated up to the level of the county. The *Common Core* indicates whether a school is a regular public, charter, or magnet school; its enrollment by grade; and its enrollment by racial subgroup and other subgroup (English learner, free-lunch participant, reduced-price lunch participant, special education participant). The *Com-*

mon Core does not, however, contain accurate information on enrollment in or the number of charter schools in school years up through 1999–2000. Thus, for the purposes of constructing Tables 1.1 and 1.2, the dataset was supplemented with information from U.S. Department of Education Reports (1999, 2000) and Center for Education Reform reports (2003, 2004, 2005). The published reports are based on at least as much, and more, data than are in the *Common Core*. Thus, when a report and the aggregated *Common Core* generated different statistics, the statistics from the report was kept. Upon occasion, statistics from two reports were in conflict. Because undercounting, not overcounting, plagues statistics on charter schools, the maximum enrollment or number of schools was reported where sources were conflict. Such conflicts, however, were minor in magnitude. The data are aggregated to the county level.

Data on State Charter School Laws

The data on state charter school laws are from Center for Education Reform (2003).

Data on Per-Pupil Revenue in Charter Schools

The enrollment data used for the denominator of this variable are from the 2002–03 version of the *Common Core of Data* (U.S. Department of Education, 2004). The revenue data used for the numerator are from the 2003–03 version of the *Public Elementary-Secondary Education Finance Data* (U.S. Department of Commerce, 2005). Charter school revenue and expenditure can be computed as follows. For single charter schools that are treated by their states as separate districts, a full set of revenue and expenditure figures are reported at the school level in the *Public Elementary-Secondary Education Finance Data*. For the rare charter schools that are part of a group and are treated by their states as

Appendix Table Determinants of the Number of Various Types of Charter School Students

	Dependent Variable: Natural Log of the Number of Charter School Students in a County who are . . .						
	in Grades K–5	*in Grades 6–8*	*in Grades 9–12*	*white*	*black*	*Hispanic*	*eligible for free or reduced-price lunch*
Factors that Mainly Affect Charter School Supply							
ln(Charter School Revenue Per Pupil, in thousands)	**0.75**	**0.55**	**0.59**	**0.39**	**0.41**	**0.70**	**1.06**
Years Since Charter Law Passed	**0.82**	**0.97**	**0.54**	**0.92**	0.21	**0.44**	0.43
Fiscal Autonomy (1–5 scale)	**0.78**	0.34	**4.25**	−0.49	**2.82**	**1.08**	−0.97
Autonomy at Start-Up (1–5 Scale)	**0.60**	**0.99**	**−1.30**	**0.77**	−0.24	0.01	**1.06**
Legal/Operational Autonomy (1–5 scale)	**−1.83**	**−1.77**	**−1.64**	**−1.05**	**−1.95**	**−1.22**	−1.09
Guaranteed Full Per-Pupil Funding (1–5 scale)	**0.82**	**1.06**	**−1.13**	**0.78**	0.08	0.26	**1.09**
Factors that Mainly Affect the Demand for Charter Schools							
ln(black students in county)	**0.43**	**0.64**	**0.70**	**0.28**	**1.23**	**0.26**	0.42
ln(Hispanic students in county)	**−0.26**	0.11	**0.39**	−0.16	−0.12	**0.87**	0.10
ln(White students in county)	0.32	**0.75**	**0.94**	**0.68**	−0.07	−0.20	**−0.87**
ln(Asian students in county)	**−0.28**	−0.27	−0.23	−0.12	−0.31	−0.27	−0.49

ln(households with income less than $30,000)	0.19	0.38	−0.22	−0.26	0.57	−0.25	0.59
ln(magnet school students in county)	−0.06	**−0.07**	**−0.06**	0.00	−0.03	−0.01	0.03
Index of Choice among Public Schl Districts (0–1 scale)	**−1.24**	**−1.26**	−0.86	**−1.13**	**−1.06**	−0.50	**−0.45**
ln(special education students in county)	**0.92**	−0.49	0.05	0.62	0.20	**0.69**	**0.89**
ln(English language learners in county)	**0.10**	0.03	−0.07	−0.01	0.09	0.01	0.35
Factors that Affect Both Supply and Demand							
large city	**−0.02**	**−0.02**	**−0.03**	−0.01	**−0.07**	0.00	**0.06**
mid-sized city	**−0.05**	−0.08	0.06	**−0.03**	−0.05	0.03	**0.10**
urban fringe of a large city	−0.07	0.24	**−0.55**	−0.08	−0.25	**−0.28**	**−0.54**
urban fringe of a mid-sized city	−0.04	0.28	**−0.63**	−0.04	−0.32	**−0.33**	**−0.56**
large town	**−0.08**	**−0.09**	−0.05	**−0.06**	**−0.18**	**0.04**	0.12
small town	−0.12	−0.06	−0.08	−0.04	−0.12	0.02	0.09
rural but inside metropolitan statistical area	**0.17**	**0.39**	−0.07	0.23	0.00	**−0.12**	0.05
rural and outside metropolitan statistical area	0.03	−0.07	**0.23**	**0.17**	0.11	0.13	**0.55**
constant	**−17.54**	**−21.53**	**−13.13**	**−14.63**	**−12.72**	**−9.34**	**−10.38**

Notes: The table shows estimates from linear regressions. Because the dependent variables are in natural log units, one may interpret the coefficient as the *percentage change effect* of the explanatory variable. If the explanatory variable is also in natural log units, then one may interpret the coefficient as the percentage change effect of a percentage change effect in the explanatory variable. A coefficient that is shown in bold typeface is statistically significantly different from zero at the 0.20 level. The standard errors were computed to be robust with clustering at the level of the state. The variables that are measured on a scale of 1 to 5 are such that a higher value corresponds to more of the property in question—for instance, *more* fiscal autonomy. See Table 1.3 and data appendix for details on variables.

a district, a full set of revenue and expenditure figures are reported at group (of charter schools) level in the *Public Elementary-Secondary Education Finance Data*. For charter schools that are dependent on a regular public school district and receive revenue only from it, the *Public Elementary-Secondary Education Finance Data* report the funds transferred from the overseeing district and received by the charter school. Thus, in order to compute charter schools' revenue, each charter school is first classified (independent, dependent; single, part of a group) and then the correct revenue and expenditure measures are associated with each school. The data are aggregated to the county level.

Other Data

The index of choice among public school districts is a standard index of deconcentration. To compute it, each school district's share of enrollment in the county is calculated. Each enrollment share is squared, and the sum of the squared shares is calculated. The sum is subtracted from 1. Enrollment data from the *Common Core* (as described above) is used.

The share of households with incomes less than $30,000 in 1999 is taken from the *School District Demographics* data, which are at the district level, and aggregated to the county level.

The share of teachers who are union members is taken from the 1987 *Census of Governments* (U.S. Department of Commerce, 1990), the most recent census of teachers unionization. The data are collected at the district level; they are aggregated to the county level for the purpose of this paper.

2. Charter School Funding

Eric Osberg

Among the many debates among charter school supporters and their opponents, perhaps none is more contentious than that over funding. Charter school leaders and their advocates claim that charters receive less than their fair share of education funds—that is, less than district schools receive. Opponents counter that charters actually receive more funding than their district counterparts, and in the process strain district budgets. Questions about whether charter and district schools serve similar students and incur similar expenses further complicate these arguments. Where does the truth lie? This chapter examines charter school funding nationwide in an attempt to separate fact from fiction.

Previous Research

There has long been anecdotal evidence of a disparity in funding between charters and traditional district schools. Charter leaders have occasionally complained of perceived shortfalls, though perhaps few have listened. Private foundations working with charter schools have noticed great need among their grantees, as have others working with charters, and see that they often operate on shoestring budgets. However, only a smattering of research reports has confirmed that district schools receive more funding, per pupil, than do charter schools.

In 2003, the American Federation of Teachers (AFT) released a large report covering eleven states, entitled *Paying for the Vision: Charter School Revenues and Expenditures*. It found that the gap between charter and district school funding ranged from $549 to $1,841 per pupil (based on data from 1997–98 and 1998–99, depending on the state).[1] In that same year, RAND studied California charters, and while they did not offer much comparative data on funding, they provided insights nonetheless, reporting that "[c]harter schools have significantly lower participation than conventional public schools in categorical aid programs outside the block grant," and "[t]he majority of charter schools are struggling with acquiring and financing facilities."[2]

In 2004, researchers at New York University's Steinhardt School of Education concluded that a typical charter school in New York State serving a typical set of students might receive 7.2 percent less funding than traditional public schools (and 14.5 percent less in revenue per se, excluding "in-kind" services received from the school district). Among elementary schools this gap reached 9.5 percent, and among schools educating full-time special education students it amounted to as much as 24.2 percent. The authors aptly concluded, "If charter schools are to have a fair opportunity to provide new, high quality educational alternatives for the public school students of New York State, these differences should be eliminated."[3]

1. "Paying for the Vision: Charter School Revenues and Expenditures," F. Howard Nelson, Edward Muir, and Rachel Drown, American Federation of Teachers, May 2003.

2. "Charter School Operations and Performance," RAND Education, 2003, pps. 113–114. http://www.rand.org/publications/MR/MR1700/.

3. Robin Jacobowitz and Jonathan S. Gyruko, *Charter School Funding in New*

Finally, in 2004 the Thomas B. Fordham Institute—sister organization to the Thomas B. Fordham Foundation—commissioned a study from Public Impact's Bryan Hassel and Michelle Terrell. Their short analysis found that Dayton's charters in 2001–02 received $7,510 per pupil, compared to $10,802 for district schools—a shortfall of 30 percent.[4] A small portion of this $3,300 gap—$421—is attributable to differences in the types of students served by district and charter schools in Dayton. However, the bulk of the gap cannot be explained by any such reason—district schools simply received more funding than charters.

However, none of these studies, or the few others not mentioned above, could be called definitive on the question of whether charter schools receive less funding than district schools. Several of them are purely regional in emphasis, so one might learn about Ohio or California but not about Arizona, Michigan, or other states with significant numbers of charter schools. Others, such as NYU's study of New York and the AFT's *Venturesome Capital* (the precursor to its 2003 report mentioned above), study charter laws and funding formulae to determine how much funding one would *expect* charters to receive. As explained below, reality does not always meet expectations in charter funding, so it is important that studies be based on funding data, not funding formulas.

Given the growth of the charter school movement, it is also important to base any study on data that are as current as possible. What was true at the beginning of the charter school movement may not be applicable today, as the charters blossomed and

York: Perspectives on Parity with Traditional Public Schools, Institute for Education and Social Policy, Steinhardt School of Education, New York University, March 2004.

4. Bryan C. Hassel and Michelle Godard Terrell, *School Finance in Dayton: A Comparison of the Revenues of the School District and Community Schools* (Chapel Hill: Public Impact, March 2004). http://www.edexcellence.net/foundation/publication/publication.cfm?id=330.

school funding in general grew. The largest study to date—the AFT's—used data from 1997–98 and 1998–99. Certainly much could have changed since that time.

Recent Research

A clear picture of charter school funding emerges when one examines some of the most recent data available—for the 2002–03 school year—in sixteen prominent charter school states and the District of Columbia (selected for either the number of charter students in that state or the quality of their charter school law).[5] These states, including D.C., for these purposes, contained over 2,200 charter schools in 2002–03, far more than any prior study has included. According to the Center for Education Reform's statistics, these states enroll 84 percent of American's charter school students.

These funding data include all revenues received by both district and charter schools in 2002–03 regardless of their sources—federal, state, local, or even philanthropic funds—and regardless of their purpose—for daily operations, facilities, or start-up costs. In this way no receipts are uncounted and one can fairly compare charter and district school funding. These data also include all charter and district schools in operation in those seventeen states, even though the presence of some charter schools in their first year of operations might skew the results—for example, if a re-

5. The data analyzed here were predominately collected for a project of the Thomas B. Fordham Institute: "Charter School Funding: Inequity's Next Frontier," by Sheree Speakman, Bryan Hassel, and Chester E. Finn, Jr., published by the Thomas B. Fordham Institute, August 2005. The study covered 2002–03 data, the most recent year available, and unless otherwise indicated all the figures discussed here refer to that year. In five states, reliable statewide figures on both charter and district revenues were unavailable. In those states, the study relies on more reliable numbers from the state's large districts to estimate the charter-district differential. See http://www.edexcellence.net/institute/charterfinance/ for additional details.

Table 2.1 State Disparities between Charter and District Funding, 2002–03

Gap/State	*District PPR*	*Charter PPR*	*Variance*	*Percent Variance*
Approaching Parity				
Minnesota	$10,056	$10,302	$245	2.4%
New Mexico	$9,020	$8,589	($430)	−4.8%
Moderate				
North Carolina	$7,465	$7,051	($414)	−5.5%
Florida	$7,831	$6,936	($896)	−11.4%
Michigan	$9,199	$8,031	($1,169)	−12.7%
Texas	$8,456	$7,300	($1,155)	−13.7%
Large				
Colorado	$10,270	$8,363	($1,908)	−18.6%
Arizona	$8,503	$6,771	($1,732)	−20.4%
New York	$13,291	$10,548	($2,743)	−20.6%
Washington, D.C.	$16,117	$12,565	($3,552)	−22.0%
Illinois	$8,801	$6,779	($2,023)	−23.0%
Severe				
Missouri	$12,640	$9,003	($3,638)	−28.8%
Wisconsin (estimated*)	$10,283	$7,250	($3,034)	−29.5%
Georgia (estimated*)	$7,406	$5,125	($2,281)	−30.8%
Ohio (estimated*)	$8,193	$5,629	($2,564)	−31.3%
California (estimated*)	$7,058	$4,835	($2,223)	−31.5%
South Carolina (estimated*)	$8,743	$5,289	($3,453)	−39.5%
State Average (weighted by charter enrollment)	$8,504	$6,704	($1,801)	−21.7%

*In five states, we were unable to obtain statewide data on charter and/or district revenues. In those states, we used data from large districts as a proxy. Full details on this calculation appear in the methodology section and the state chapters.

cently-opened school received a start-up grant but had few students. The only schools excluded are those without reliable data.

The results of such an analysis are striking (table 2.1). In these seventeen states, charter schools faced an average funding shortfall of $1,801 per pupil in 2002–03. While a district school could expect to receive $8,504 per student, a charter could only count on $6,704, a difference of 21.7 percent. Nine states faced much worse shortfalls, ranging as high as $3,638 per pupil in Missouri.

The most egregious gaps, in percentage terms, existed in

Georgia, Ohio, California and South Carolina, where charter schools could expect to receive only two-thirds of the resources of district schools. The gaps occurred in large charter states like Arizona, with 457 charters operating in 2002–03, and small charter states like Illinois, with just twenty-two charter schools. In only two states did funding approach "parity" between charter and district schools, and in those (Minnesota and New Mexico) non-recurring start-up funds for charter schools may have contributed to the results. Nowhere can one safely conclude that a state funded charters perfectly fairly. Indeed, the pattern is clear—inequity was the norm.

The situation appears even worse when one examines the large urban districts within those seventeen states, suggesting that the neediest of students are (perhaps not surprisingly) subject to the greatest hardships (table 2.2). Among twenty-seven large districts, the average funding gap between charter and district schools in 2002–03 was $2,256 per pupil, or 23.5 percent. Charters in Atlanta, San Diego and Greenville, South Carolina—cities with the largest gaps—were expected to make do with only three-fifths of the per pupil revenue of a typical district school. In Albany, charters received nearly $5,000 less per pupil than their district counterparts.

Since charter-district comparisons within a single district are more likely to be among similar types of schools, serving comparable types of students (whereas comparisons within a state as a whole can encompass diverse areas, such as urban and rural districts), it appears fair to conclude that this larger district-level gap of 23.5 percent is most indicative of the degree to which charter schools are shortchanged nationwide.

In absolute dollars, the funding a charter school can expect to receive varies greatly from state to state. But funding gaps create significant challenges for charter schools everywhere. They must buy goods and services in the same local economy as do

Table 2.2 State Disparities between Charter and District Funding, 2002–03

Gap/District	*District PPR*	*Charter PPR*	*Variance*	*Percent Variance*
Approaching Parity				
Albuquerque, NM	$7,745	$8,511	$766	9.9%
Moderate				
St. Paul, MN	$11,876	$10,800	($1,076)	−9.1%
Denver, CO	$9,954	$8,755	($1,199)	−12.0%
New York City, NY	$12,505	$10,881	($1,624)	−13,0%
Dallas, TX	$8,300	$7,125	($1,174)	−14.2%
Large				
Detroit, MI	$9,899	$8,395	($1,504)	−15.2%
Minneapolis, MN	$13,701	$11,575	($2,127)	−15.5%
Houston, TX	$7,724	$6,382	($1,341)	−17.4%
Broward Co., FL	$7,669	$6,273	($1,396)	−18.2%
Miami-Dade, FL	$7,971	$6,465	($1,506)	−18.9%
Fulton Co., GA	$11,748	$9,325	($2,423)	−20.6%
Washington, D.C.	$16,117	$12,565	($3,552)	−22.0%
Buffalo, NY	$13,197	$10,211	($2,986)	−22.6%
Chicago, IL	$8,907	$6,847	($2,060)	−23.1%
Severe				
Maricopa Co., AZ	$8,743	$6,389	($2,354)	−26.9%
Colorado Springs, CO	$8,401	$6,100	($2,301)	−27.4%
St. Louis, MO	$12,531	$9,035	($3,495)	−27.9%
Cleveland, OH	$10,732	$7,704	($3,028)	−28.2%
Los Angeles, CA	$7,960	$5,653	($2,307)	−29.0%
Milwaukee, WI	$11,267	$7,944	($3,323)	−29.5%
Wake Co., NC	$9,237	$6,510	($2,727)	−29.5%
Kansas City, MO	$12,795	$8,990	($3,806)	−29.7%
Albany, NY	$15,226	$10,235	($4,991)	−32.8%
Dayton, OH	$11,498	$7,614	($3,884)	−33.8%
Atlanta, GA	$12,766	$7,949	($4,818)	−37.7%
Greenville, SC	$8,477	$5,126	($3,351)	−39.5%
San Diego, CA	$8,333	$4,964	($3,369)	−40.4%
District Average (weighted by charter enrollment)	$9,604	$7,348	($2,256)	−23.5%

much better-funded district schools. Charters in San Diego, for example, made do with just $4,964 per pupil in 2002–03, (compared to district schools' $8,333) while their counterparts in Washington, D.C. received a relatively generous $12,565 per pupil (compared to district schools' $16,117). The higher absolute amount in Washington helps explain its wealth of charter schools—in 2005–06, it has fifty-two schools serving 24 percent of the District's public school students.[6] Thus it is important to evaluate charter funding not simply relative to district funding, but also in terms of differentiations in absolute amounts provided. States that provide charter schools the least money cannot expect national charter management organizations—source of many charter success stories—to develop large numbers of schools there.

Critics have argued that the data showing charter funding disparities are misleading because districts sometimes provide services to charters, such as transportation or the central administration of a special education program, and pay for these services from their own budgets. In some instances, this does happen. But it is also true that districts can withhold funds from charters for services they do not need (more on this below). In some states charters must pay a fee to their authorizers. Thus the fundamental conclusion that charter schools are inequitably funded relative to district schools is unchanged.

A funding gap of $1,800 per pupil is large enough to affect the operations of a school. Consider a typical 250-student charter school. It could expect to receive $450,000 less than a similar district school—each year. After a few years, such a school would find itself cumulatively behind by millions of dollars. One can imagine what a charter school might do with such funds—hire ten teachers, create a science lab, stock its library shelves, start an after-school program. The list is endless, but it is clear that this gap is significant—and that closing it even partially might make a difference in the achievement of the students attending these schools.

6. Jay Mathews, "Why Did I Ignore Charter Schools?" *Washington Post*, September 27, 2005, http://www.washingtonpost.com/wp-dyn/content/article/2005/09/27/AR2005092700603.html.

What Explains These Results?

One must consider the possibility that differences in the students served by charter and district schools explain the funding disparities. If district schools serve proportionally more poor students, special education students, or high school students, then they would be justified in receiving more funding. Such students are more expensive to educate, and most funding formulae give them greater weight. However, closer examination shows that student characteristics could not have explained these large gaps—though they could account for part of the disparity in some states.

To understand the potential impact of serving poor students, one can examine free lunch eligibility. In most of these seventeen states in 2002–03, charter and district schools served comparable percentages of poor students. In a few, such as Arizona, D.C., Michigan, New York and Texas, charters served considerably more, and in these states charter schools received less funding despite serving a more needy (and expensive to educate) population.

Only in Colorado, Florida, South Carolina and Wisconsin did district schools serve proportionally more free-lunch eligible students, and analysis shows that these discrepancies could only marginally affect the funding gaps we found. For example, in 2002–03 South Carolina exhibited large differences in the percentage of students eligible for free and reduced price lunch, with 36.2 percent of district students and just 10.7 percent of charter students eligible. Comparing two hypothetical 250-student charter and district schools, the district school is likely to serve approximately sixty-four more free-lunch eligible students than the charter school. If these students each carried an additional $2,000 in funding, the district school would receive $128,000 more than the charter. However, the real funding gap is $863,000 with district school's failure. Student poverty accounts for less than 15 percent of the total funding gap between the two schools. In other words, the more needy population in district schools can account for less than one-sixth of the funding gap.

Similar conclusions arise when glancing at grade levels served, though this is more difficult to analyze because so many charter schools operate non-traditional grade configurations (such as K–12 or K–8). Finally, though special education data were not available on a state-by-state basis for 2002–03, SRI has shown that charter schools typically serve a lower percentage of special education students than do district schools—9 percent versus 12 percent.[7] Such a difference would affect funding, but should not account for more than a slight portion of the funding gaps described above. Consider again two 250-student schools. If 99 percent of the charter students and 12 percent of the district students were classified special education, the difference would be eight students. If each special education student received an additional $8,000 in funding (a reasonable approximation of the additional funding available to special education students),[8] the per-pupil funding for the district school as a whole would rise by $256, or

7. "Evaluation of the Public Charter Schools Program: Final Report," SRI International, July 2004; http://www.sri.com/news/releases/12-09-02.html.

8. In 2002 the President's Commission on Excellence in Special Education reported that in 1999–2000, "total spending used to educate the average student with a disability was an estimated $12,639. This amount includes $8,080 per pupil on special education services, $4,394 per pupil on regular education services and $165 per pupil on services from other federal, special needs programs." (See "A New Era: Revitalizing Special Education for Children and Their Families," President's Commission on Special Education, July 1, 2002, p. 30. http://www.ed.gov/inits/commisionsboards/whspecialeducation/index.html.)The Commission also reported that "the U.S. Department of Education now estimates that, as a nation, we are spending about 90% (1.9 times) more on the average eligible student for special education than we do on the average general education student with no special needs." (p. 31) Ninety percent of the average charter school per-pupil funding ($6,704) would be $6,034 and of the average district per-pupil funding ($8,504) would be $7,654. Thus $8,000 is an appropriate approximation for the simple analysis presented above.

just 14 percent of the $1,801 funding gap observed between charter and district schools.

Thus one can be skeptical of claims that district schools deserve greater funding than charter schools because of differences in students served. On average, charters are overwhelmingly under-funded in comparison to district schools, even when considering the types of students they serve.

Why is this so? There are a number of important reasons, many of them rooted in state policy. The most important reasons are examined below.

Local Funding

It is essential to compare charter and district funding by source—that is, according to whether the funds come from the state (by formulas or programs), federal government programs, private philanthropy, or local sources of revenue. Comparison makes it clear that local funds are an important contributor to the charter school funding shortfall. Generally speaking, district schools receive a full "share" of local funds while charter schools receive considerably less. Districts can, and often do, levy taxes to pay for parts of their operations, and these funds are not all shared with charters. In many of the seventeen states in table 2.1, this is the primary cause of the discrepancy between district and charter funding.

To illustrate this point, one can plot the relationship between the share of local funding in a state—that is, the percentage of school funding supported by local dollars—and the gap between district and charter funding. The resulting graph (fig. 2.1) reveals a powerful relationship.

Though this analysis is admittedly based on a small number of observations, a pattern is evident. It indicates that 73 percent of the gap between charter and district funding is related to the

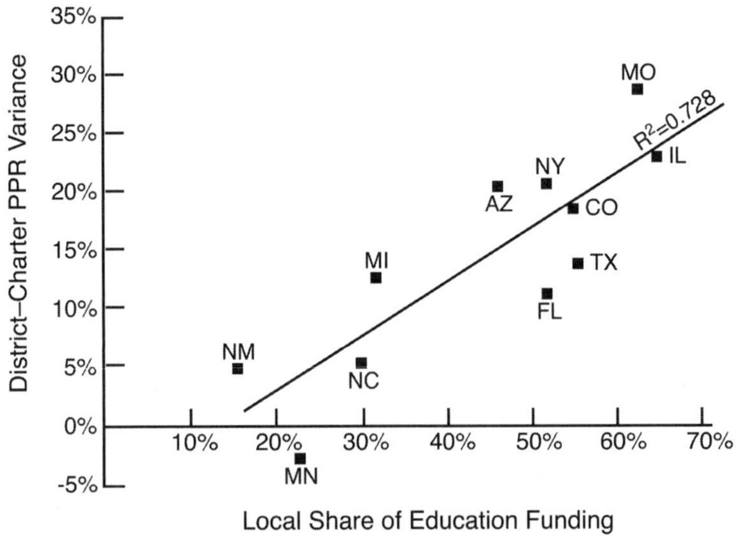

Fig. 2.1 Relationship between Local Funding and the Charter Funding Shortfall

Each state is represented by a point, with the state's charter funding shortfall (as a percentage) on the vertical axis and the portion of school funding that comes from local sources on the horizontal axis.

state's reliance on local funding of education. In Missouri and Illinois, for example, district schools relied on local funding for over 50 percent of their funding, and the charter funding shortfalls were 29 percent and 23 percent, respectively.

States often recognize this problem and attempt to rectify it; in about half of these seventeen states, charters received a greater share of state funding than did district schools. For example, in 2002–03 Arizona offered district schools between $3,208 and $3,390 per pupil in state funding (varying depending on enrollment and grade level), which, when added to certain program grants, brought total state funding for district schools to $3,770 per pupil on average. Recognizing that district schools received more local funding (about $3,000 per pupil more) than charters, Arizona offered charter schools about $5,400 per pupil—an advantage of $1,600 per pupil. However, this additional state funding only offsets half the shortfall in local funding, ultimately leaving charter schools about 20 percent poorer than district schools.

Similar situations occur in other states, and the example of North Carolina shows that it is possible to minimize the impact of local revenues on the charter funding gap. There, policymakers have addressed the problem, as the state requires local districts to pay charters their *full* share of local funding. The process appears to work reasonably well; charters received just $200 less in local funding per pupil than district schools, and the total funding gap was just 5.5 percent (about $400).

Facilities Funding

Most charters are denied facilities funding. This problem is intertwined with their lack of access to local funding, because facilities funding often derives from local sources. Only seven of the seventeen states had laws on the books in 2002–03 providing charters access to facilities funding sources enjoyed by districts. In only five of these did charters receive such funds in practice, and never in amounts equal to that received by district schools.

The District of Columbia, however, demonstrates that solutions to the facilities funding challenge are possible. D.C. offers charters a facilities allotment that is designed to mirror the amount given to district schools. It is not necessarily perfect—it calculates the charter funding amount based on a rolling five-year average of district funding, so if district spending rises over time charters will lag behind—but it is a reasonable solution.[9] Other states are improving charter facilities funding, to varying degrees. Minnesota, for example, offers charter schools substantial "lease

9. In 2002–03, per-pupil charter facility funding in the District of Columbia trailed the district school amount, as facility funding for district schools that year exceeded the average of the five prior years.

aid" to cover the costs of renting buildings. California earmarked $400 million from a state facilities bond for charter schools (though as of 2002–03, charters had received none of these funds). New York City recently released a five-year capital plan that includes $350 million for charter schools.[10] Georgia created a needs-based facilities fund for charter schools that it funded with just $500,000 for 2005–06. Obviously such a small amount cannot fund the needs of an entire state; yet Georgia's offering is more than most states provide. More legislators should follow the lead of policymakers like those in D.C. and aim for parity in facilities funding between charter and district schools.

Local Education Agency Status

Many federal and certain state education funding programs are designed to route money through a Local Education Agency (LEA)—that is, the school district. Districts apply on behalf of their schools and control the funds they receive. Such a process can easily exclude charter schools. Only four of these seventeen states had the foresight to designate charter schools as LEAs for the purpose of receiving federal funds. Seven other states treat their charters as LEAs in some circumstances but not in others; Texas, for example, allows its charters to apply as LEAs for federal funds but not for certain state funds (such as "Small District Adjustment" funds, for which charters are typically small enough to otherwise qualify). Charters without LEA status rely on the local district to apply on their behalf for certain funds, and districts can often retain a portion of the funding to cover their administrative expenses (whether or not the charters benefited from any services).

This seemingly minor administrative detail has big conse-

10. 2005–2009 "Children First" Five-Year Capital Plan Overview, available at http://www.nycsca.org/pdf/capitalplanoutline.pdf.

quences. Among the states that grant full LEA status to charters are Minnesota (where charters received $1,083 per pupil in federal funding) and the District of Columbia ($1,448); those states which do not do so include Colorado ($273), Florida ($463), and Illinois ($395), among others.

A charter school (or district) with LEA status does take on a greater responsibility to educate special education students, as the Individuals with Disabilities Education Act (IDEA) tasks the LEA with the responsibility to ensure that all students receive a "free appropriate public education" (FAPE).[11] Thus one might argue that the fact that some charter schools are not considered LEAs, and thus face fewer IDEA obligations than their district counterparts, justifies a difference in funding between district and charter schools. However, as the hypothetical situation discussed earlier demonstrates, differences in special education populations can account for only a small portion of the funding gap observed in these seventeen states.

Circuitous Funding of Charter Schools

These funding challenges are exacerbated when charters do not receive their revenues directly from the state, but rather have it channeled through the district first. Only four of the seventeen states avoid this problem; charters in the remaining states face this situation to a certain extent (the specifics of which vary from state to state). New Hampshire, though not among the states in table 2.1, offers a vivid example. In the summer of 2005, one of the Granite State's original charter schools was told it could not reopen because the local district had decided to withhold its funding. As the *Portsmouth Herald* reported, "Under the state's charter school law, the only funds the state is mandated to pro-

11. For an explanation of these responsibilities see, for example, http://www.uscharterschools.org/cs/spedp/view/sped_aud/3?x-t=bkgd.view.

vide for a school is the $3,340 per student allotted for an 'adequate education.' The funds pass through local school districts to the charter schools. But the school district, and later the Franklin City Council, refused to pass on the money," with "the Franklin City Council . . . saying it is needed for local public schools."[12] The school is now closed for at least a year. Though the state has ordered the city council to send the funds owed to the charter school, it has yet to do so.[13] In another case in Kansas City, a judge must rule on the district's decision to withhold $45 million in funding that charter schools claim is due to them. The district argues it needs the funds to improve its facilities, in accordance with a desegregation ruling, and a resolution is still pending.[14]

Violations of Legislative Intent

Even when legislators appear to have intended for charters to receive their fair share of funding, they can be denied dollars in practice. Fifteen of the seventeen states specify in their statutes that charters should have access to federal funds, but in practice charters in only seven of these states get access to the same federal dollars as their district counterparts. Similarly, every state law indicates that charters should receive state funding, but in eight of the states charters did not have the same access as district schools. And as described above, the problems are most pronounced with local and facilities funding. In no state do charters receive their fair share of either, though nine of seventeen states

12. Kathleen D. Bailey, "Charter schools minus one in New Hampshire," *The Portsmouth Herald*, July 17, 2005. http://www.seacoastonline.com/news/07172005/news/53167.htm.

13. Melanie Asmar, "Voters pick four newcomers," *Concord Monitor*, October 5, 2005. http://www.concordmonitor.com/apps/pbcs.dll/article?AID=/20051005/REPOSITORY/510050365/1001/NEWS01.

14. Deanne Smith, "Judge rejects most of KC schools' case," *Kansas City Star*, July 27, 2005.

intend, through state law, for charters to receive local funding, and seven states allow for facilities funding.

Georgia provides a good example of how actual funding practices can stray far from the intent of the charter law. The Georgia Charter Schools Act specifically states that, "The local board and the state board shall treat a start-up charter school no less favorably than other local schools within the applicable local system with respect to the provision of funds for instruction and school administration and, where feasible, transportation, food services, and building programs."[15] Unfortunately, in reality, "this clause has allowed districts to fund charter school expenses on a selective basis. Most districts withhold a portion of per-pupil dollars to pay for central administration, school nutrition, transportation, and other expenses, whether or not a charter schools requires (or wants) these services."[16]

Complexities of School Funding

Some of the under-funding of charter schools occurs because state finance systems are complex and have existed for years to serve a system of school districts, not an innovation like charter schools. Charters, which by their nature are designed to exist outside the school system, can only integrate seamlessly if legislatures take care to ensure that *all* relevant laws and regulations are adapted as necessary to accommodate these new organizations. Arizona's experience with the federal Department of Education offers an example of this problem. Due to a definition of a "public" school that precludes those operated by for-profit organizations, as is

15. Georgia Charter Schools Act of 1997, http://www.legis.state.ga.us/legis/1997_98/leg/fulltext/hb353.htm.

16. Sheree Speakman, Bryan Hassel, and Chester E. Finn, Jr., "Charter School Funding: Inequity's Next Frontier," Thomas B. Fordham Institute, August 2005, p. 56.

common in Arizona, the Department of Education ruled in March, 2005, that such charters in that state were ineligible for federal funds.[17] Bureaucratic rules sometimes trump common sense.

Many charters are overwhelmed by the paperwork and compliance challenges of applying for federal funds. RAND's 2003 study of California charter schools noted that "Charter school operators are often unsophisticated in completing the forms and carrying out the procedural activities that have taken districts years to master," and that charter schools may not have the "economies of scale" that districts enjoy.[18] A 2003 study by Policy Analysis for California Education (PACE) illustrates the results: 43 percent of charter students in 1999 were eligible for free or reduced-price lunch, though only 4.5 percent of them actually received "support funded through federal Title I dollars."[19] Certainly not all of this difference is due to thoughtless rules or laws that advantage district schools over charters. School funding systems nationwide set up many hoops through which all public schools—both district and charter—must jump, but such rules of the game particularly hamper charter schools, which are less experienced, smaller, and often grappling with the challenges of starting up. They advantage district schools, experienced in the mazes of bureaucracy. Education financing is in drastic need of a major simplification for the benefit of all schools, but especially for charter schools.

17. Editorial, "Educrats in Washington Take a Shot at School Choice," *East Valley Tribune*, June 26, 2005. http://www.edreform.com/index.cfm?fuseAction=document&documentID=2096&sectionID=58.

18. "Charter School Operations and Performance," RAND Education, 2003, p. 91. http://www.rand.org/publications/MR/MR1700/.

19. "Charter Schools and Inequality: National Disparities in Funding, Teacher Quality, and Student Support," Policy Analysis for California Education, April 2003.

Tactics of Charter Opponents

Many of charter schools' funding ills arise neither from bureaucratic hassles nor well-intentioned but poorly implemented laws. Charter opponents work to ensure that charters will be weak, and they fight vigorously against any reforms that might make charter schools a greater threat to them. Districts themselves are complicit as well, and not just by participating in some of the funding shenanigans described above. When charter laws are debated, districts often complain loudly that "their" funds will be sent to charter schools. Sometimes such complaints result in "hold harmless" clauses, whereby the financial impact of charters on districts is diminished or phased in over time. In Illinois, for example, the state reimburses districts for the impact of charter schools on a graduated scale—offering them 90 percent of the funds used by charters in their first year, 65 percent in their second and 35 percent in their third. Such arrangements prevent funding from truly following the student and perpetuate the gap between charter and district schools.

Worse still, when charters act rationally in response to tight budgets—perhaps hiring younger, less expensive teachers—they are subject to criticism for shortchanging their students. Charter schools have not typically been well organized to respond. Though charter leaders and their associations bemoan the lack of funding, they often lack specific data to bolster their claims, and their pleas can be denigrated as self-interested. Hopefully shedding light on the charter school funding problem will clarify this debate and enable decisions about school finance to be based on facts rather than hyperbole.

Overcoming Funding Inequities

The gap in funding between charter and district schools is significant and has many roots, but many charters do their best to make up the gap. Some seek private funding for facilities, but banks often view them as risky—particularly because, unlike their district counterparts, charter schools can be closed. In its report debunking this perception of risk, the Kauffman Foundation laments that "Low-cost, charity-rate loans and mortgages for large amounts are scarce. And on the conventional market, charter schools tend to encounter additional charges rather than discounts."[20]

Others seek philanthropic support for their schools. The funding disparities in table 2.1—an average gap of over $1,800 per pupil—exist even *after* factoring in charters' ability to find private donors willing to supplement public funding. It is inconceivable that charters could raise sufficient additional grants, beyond the philanthropy they already receive, in order to eliminate their shortfalls. In the seventeen states for which we have data, philanthropy is limited; in 2002–03, it totaled less than $100 million,[21] quite a small portion of the $1 billion dollar gap that existed that year—or the nearly $2 billion gap that likely exists in 2005–06 across all charter states (assuming the charter-district funding gap remains at $1,800 per pupil and using the generally accepted estimate of one million charter students).

Even if fundraising could substantially reduce the funding gap, it would be an imperfect solution. Raising money is time

20. "Debunking the Real Estate Risk of Charter Schools," Ewing Marion Kauffman Foundation, 2005.

21. Researchers for "Charter School Funding: Inequity's Next Frontier," could not entirely separate philanthropic funds from certain "other" revenue sources, so an exact total is unavailable. Total "other" sources, including philanthropy, amounted to $93 million in those 17 states in 2002–03.

consuming, distracting school leaders from their priorities. It can also corrupt, causing a school to shift its priorities merely to accommodate the whims of a funder. Perhaps most importantly, it is unreliable—though some funders do offer multi-year grants, donations are inevitably short-lived and cannot be counted on to sustain a school's operations forever. Managing a school under such uncertainty adds to the challenges charters school leaders face.

Changes to state laws represent the only viable long-term solution to these funding problems. Fortunately, some states are improving their policies. California, for example, passed Assembly Bill 740 in September of 2005, combining twenty-eight categorical programs, for which charter schools previously had to apply one by one, into a single block grant. This followed the recommendation of the Legislative Analyst's Office that combining these programs "would result in charter schools being able to access more categorical funding" and "would thereby address the current discrepancy in state funding between charter schools and other public schools."[22] Charter supporters in California doubt that this will be enough to level the playing field between charter and district schools,[23] and it remains to be seen whether it works in practice as intended. However, it is encouraging that policymakers in California have taken a step to address this longstanding problem.

One can hope that all states will gradually improve their charter laws; perhaps funding gaps are merely growing pains for the charter school movement, and they will narrow over time. Unfortunately, the data provide no evidence of this. If we plot state-level funding gaps against the years in which each state passed its

22. "Assessing California's Charter Schools," Legislative Analyst's Office, January 20, 2004.

23. Kenneth Todd Ruiz, "Charter School Funding Simplified," *Inland Valley Daily Bulletin*, October 6, 2005.

initial charter school law, no discernable pattern emerges. Minnesota was the first charter state, in 1991, and its funding is more equitable than most. Georgia and Wisconsin, which followed shortly thereafter in 1993, still provide 30 percent less funding to their charter schools than to their district schools. Other early adopters such as Michigan (1993, 12.7 percent gap), Colorado (1993, 18.6 percent gap), and Arizona (1994, 20.4 percent gap) show similar inertia toward eliminating their funding gaps.[24]

State Policies Must Change

The lesson for charter supporters is clear: they need to become actively involved in designing and championing improved charter laws in their states. As shown above, there are numerous improvements that would help reduce the funding gap between charter and district schools. Facilities funds could be provided to charter schools, on par with district schools. Financing arrangements could be designed to be more direct, with money flowing straight to charters rather than through district schools. And charter schools could more often be given the opportunity to apply directly for all state and federal programs available to district schools.

However, as helpful as these solutions would be, they would be mere band aids on the problem of charter funding. To eliminate existing inequities, two fundamental improvements to school funding are needed. First, when funding education, states must reduce their reliance on local property taxes and increase the state-funded share. Such a change would reduce inequities between rich and poor districts, and it would also minimize the greatest source of inequity between charter and district schools: districts' unique ability to supplement their state and federal dol-

24. Center for Education Reform "Ranking Scorecard," http://www.edreform.com/_upload/ranking_chart.pdf.

lars with local tax revenues. Such revenues need not disappear—local citizens should have the right to bear new tax burdens for the benefit of their district schools—but state policy cannot be blind to this funding when establishing charter schools. States can and must design their charter funding policies so that charters either receive a full share of local funds or receive an additional amount to offset the local funding received by nearby district schools.

The second fundamental change is one that would benefit many constituencies, such as poor and disadvantaged students, as well as address charter funding inequities: states must begin to transform their finance systems to truly fund *the student*, rather than district arrangements, entrenched educational programs, or even schools. Old methods of funding no longer suffice in the education marketplace of today, where virtual schooling, inter-district choice, and charter schools are just a few of the innovations states have created to coexist with the ancient district-centered model of schooling. Today we need funding systems that allocate money by first taking into account each student's needs—i.e., adjusting a base amount of per-student funding to account for the additional expense of students with underdeveloped skills or requiring special education or English language instruction—and then ensuring that this funding *fully* follows the student to the school he or she attends, whether it be the neighborhood public school, a district option across town, or even a charter school. Much would need to change—no longer would a school be able to depend on a fixed amount of funding regardless of its enrollment, and as a result principals would be forced (and empowered) to think flexibly about the programs they offer. But the benefits would be tremendous, as resources would be allocated efficiently—to the schools that need them most, based purely on the students who attend. Some cities, such as Cincinnati, Houston and Seattle, have worked on this type of weighted-student funding, but this practice needs to transcend the district and form the core of state funding policies. Charter schools would receive fair funding as a result, as would schools of all kinds.

Conclusion

Some might argue that charters do not deserve to be funded on par with district schools: they were designed to show the way toward a better education system, with higher achievement and, ideally, less waste. Furthermore, the link between funding and educational performance is weak, at best. So cannot charter schools operate more efficiently, on less funding? Perhaps in time that will prove to be the case. Today, however, charter schools are paying high start-up costs and often must put resources into overcoming resistance from unions and school districts. It is unreasonable to expect them to both carry those burdens and provide better instruction with less money than other public schools. As this volume shows, charter opponents are well-organized and determined to end charter schools—or at least sharply contain their growth. They fight to keep charter laws weak, the regulatory burden heavy, and the caps tight. Charters are striving to prove they can out-perform traditional schools, but they start at a great disadvantage. Only if charter schools are allowed to compete on a level playing field, including fair levels of funding, will we ever know if they can out-perform traditional public schools. If policymakers don't fix the inequity in charter school funding, this promising reform is at risk.

The education of millions of children is at stake. It has long been held that all children have the same right to a high quality education, and that children in poor neighborhoods deserve no less of an education than those in better-off parts of the same district. Unfortunately, charter schools have been excluded from this reasoning. From coast to coast, they receive less funding than district schools, an inequity even more alarming given that they serve so many disadvantaged and minority children. This inequity must end, whether through improved laws, fine-tuned formulas, or even legal actions. Charter leaders and their teachers, students and parents are doing their part to reform our public school system. Now it is time for policymakers to respond in kind and ensure that charter schools remain a viable option for America's neediest students.

3. School Choice in Milwaukee Fifteen Years Later

Paul E. Peterson
with Nathan Torinus and Brad Smith

Whether or not the supply of schools can meet the parental demand for choice has been central to the school choice debate for more than a decade. Unfortunately, the two sides to the debate often carry their argument to the extreme. On the one side, one finds, to coin a term, the strict *inelasticians*: Those who assume that supply will not change in response to an increase in demand. When model builders make such an assumption, they easily reach the conclusion that choice systems will necessarily be highly stratified.[1] In fact, studies of school choice find increasing stratification

We wish to thank Mark Linnen, Elena Llaudet, and Antonio Wendland for their assistance in the preparation of this paper. I also wish to thank many in the city of Milwaukee who agreed to meet with us and provide us with information concerning the city's charter, voucher, and public schools, including Alan Borsuk, Howard Fuller, Aquine Jackson, Juanita Lee, George Mitchell, Alisia Moutry, Mike Ostermeyer, Cindy Zautcke, and Superintendent of Schools William Andrekopoulos.

1. See Charles F. Manski, "Educational Choice (Vouchers) and Social Mobility," *Economics of Education Review* 11, no. 4 (1992): 351–69. For a contrasting view see Terry M. Moe and Kenneth W. Shotts, "Computer Models of Educational Institutions: The Case of Vouchers and Social Equity," in *The Politics of Education and the New Institutionalism*, ed. William L. Boyd, Robert L. Crowson and Hanne B. Mawhinney (London: Falmer Press, 1996).

in contexts where school supply was forced to remain fixed.[2] But one cannot generalize from such situations to those where supply is allowed to fluctuate.[3]

On the other side, one finds those who might be called strict *elasticians*, those who assume that supply will increase smoothly as demand increases. Milton Friedman's essay that helped give rise to the school choice movement is an example of an elastician's argument.[4] But it is another matter to assume that supply will expand rapidly no matter what kind of school choice program is introduced, especially when that program is the outcome of political bargains and it falls well short of fulfilling the assumptions that Friedman set forth.

In practice, supply response will be affected by two major factors—(1) legal and political barriers and (2) financial incentives given to potential suppliers. To study how these two factors affect school supply, we examined the school choice innovations in the city of Milwaukee, where the first small voucher experiment began in 1990 and where much larger voucher and charter interventions have been in place since 1998. We also gathered information on the impact of the choice interventions on existing public schools.

If one can generalize from the Milwaukee experience, school supply is quite elastic, responding quickly to changes in parental demand whenever legal and political conditions are relaxed. Even if financial arrangements are considerably less than ideal, the supply grows with demand. But, whether those newly created schools provide a high-quality education is another matter.

2. Edward B. Fiske and Helen F. Ladd, *When Schools Compete: A Cautionary Tale* (Washington DC: Brookings Institution Press, 2000).

3. See, for example, Bryan C. Hassel, *The Charter School Challenge: Avoiding the Pitfalls, Fulfilling the Challenge* (Washington DC: Brookings Institution Press, 1999).

4. Milton Friedman, "The Role of Government in Education," in *Economics and the Public Interest*, ed. Robert Solo (Piscataway, NJ: Rutgers University Press, 1955).

Choice can sustain and enhance existing quality schools and it can have positive impacts on traditional public schools that must now take active steps to maintain their enrollments. But when financial arrangements are inadequate and oversight is lax, some of the new schools may be of lesser quality. As Howard Fuller, a vigorous school choice advocate who previously served as Milwaukee's public school superintendent has observed: "I don't think I [initially] understood how hard it is to create a really good school."[5]

School Choice in Milwaukee

Milwaukee has the largest, most mature system of school choice—consisting of both vouchers and charter schools—within a large American city. It began in 1990 when the state of Wisconsin established the Milwaukee Parental Choice Program (MPCP). For the first eight years, MPCP was limited to serving no more than 1.5 percent of the Milwaukee Public School (MPS) population, about 1,700 students. It was directed towards low-income families, who were given a voucher of (initially) up to $2,500 to pay the cost of sending their child to one of the participating private schools. Only a small number of private, secular schools within Milwaukee, which never numbered more than twenty-three, participated in the program. Schools could not ask parents to supplement the voucher with an additional tuition payment.

The state of Wisconsin enlarged the program in 1996 so that it could serve up to 15 percent of the MPS population, or approximately 15,000 students, and sectarian schools were, for the first time, allowed to participate. However, the program remained limited to low-income families and schools still needed

5. Alan J. Borsuk and Sarah Carr, "A Question of Accountability," *Milwaukee Journal Sentinel*, June 12, 2005.

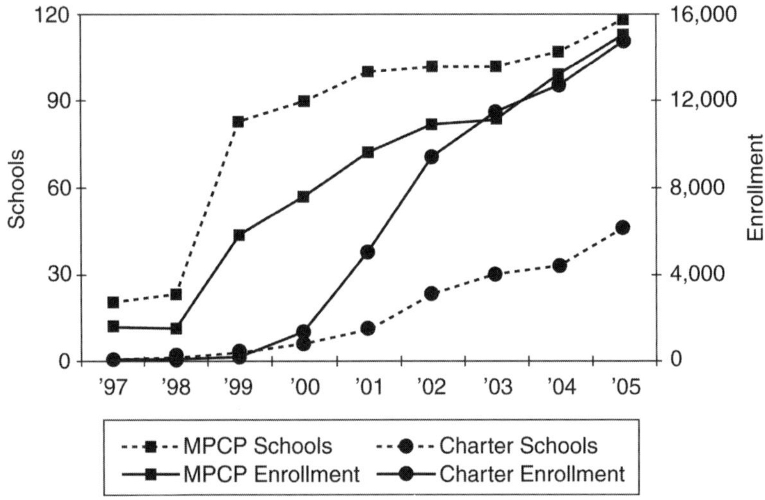

Fig. 3.1 Growth of Choice and Charter Schools in Milwaukee, 1997–2005

Sources: Wisconsin Department of Public Instruction.

to accept the voucher as the full tuition payment. The enlarged program did not become operative until the 1999 school year (a school year is identified by the chronological year in which it ends) when a lawsuit objecting to its constitutionality was rejected by Wisconsin's highest court. Ever since, any private school in Milwaukee, religious or secular, may become an MPCP member, provided its application is accepted by the state's Department of Education. Until recently, the state approved most applications.

In 2005, nearly 13,978 students, just short of the maximum allowed under the law, were accepting vouchers worth $5,943 to attend any one of 117 private schools (which in most cases also had fee-paying students as well). Those numbers represent a sharp increase from 1999 levels, when participating schools numbered eighty-six, and enrollment was just 5,800 (Figure 3.1).

Supplementing MPCP is Wisconsin's charter-school program, first set up in 1993, then enlarged in 1997. Charter schools are secular, publicly-funded schools that operate under a charter that grants them autonomy from many state and school district regulations in exchange for a commitment to fulfill the terms of their charter, which generally runs for five years. In Milwaukee, the charter may be obtained from any one of three authorizing agencies established by the state of Wisconsin—Milwaukee Public Schools (MPS), the city of Milwaukee (the city), or the University of Wisconsin-Milwaukee (UWM). By 2005, these agencies had licensed forty-five charter schools serving over 14,562 students, more than ten times the enrollment in charters only five years earlier (Figure 3.1).[6]

Of the forty-five charter schools, twenty-one (with an enrollment of 8,249) were *district-controlled schools* chartered by MPS, which have greater flexibility than traditional MPS schools but are nonetheless subject to many district regulations, including collective bargaining agreements. Thirteen (with an enrollment of 2,610) were *independent charter* schools authorized by MPS but operating free of collective bargaining contracts and most other district regulations. (In Wisconsin, the two types of schools are labeled instrumentalities and non-instrumentalities, neologisms avoided here.) The remaining eleven were independent charter schools (with an enrollment of 3,703) chartered by one of the other two authorizers.

In 2005 independent charter schools received $7,111 per pupil, nearly 20 percent more than the amount received by schools in MPCP (Figure 3.2). District-controlled charters receive the same amount as Milwaukee traditional public schools, which in 2005 was $9,024 plus the sizeable but officially undetermined

6. Milwaukee Area Technical College also has the authority to grant charters but it has not yet exercised that authority.

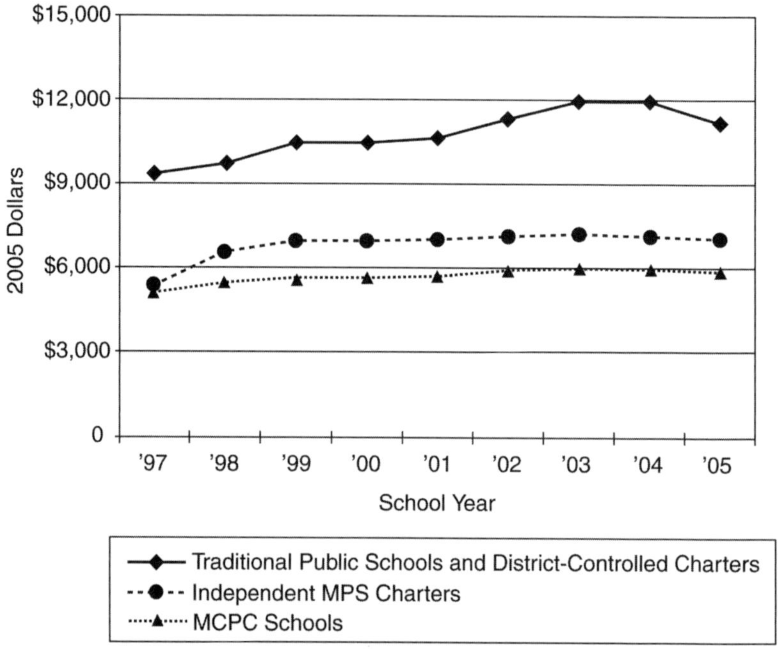

Fig. 3.2 Per-Pupil Allocation in Milwaukee Schools, 1997–2005

cost of employee pensions. Even if pension costs are set to one side, the $9,024 per pupil expenditure is 20 percent more than the amount received by independent charters and 40 percent more than the maximum amount that voucher schools could receive from the government ($5,943).

Although most choice schools have many fewer dollars per pupil than do traditional public schools in Milwaukee, the numbers of students attending choice schools has increased rapidly since 1999. By 2005, Milwaukee's voucher and charter programs were serving 28,540 students, 23.7 percent of all students being educated at public expense (Figure 3.3). Another 6,700 of the Milwaukee students chose to attend public schools outside the district, lifting the percentage of students exercising choice at the expense of traditional public schools to close to 30 percent of all publicly-funded students living in Milwaukee. That is a long dis-

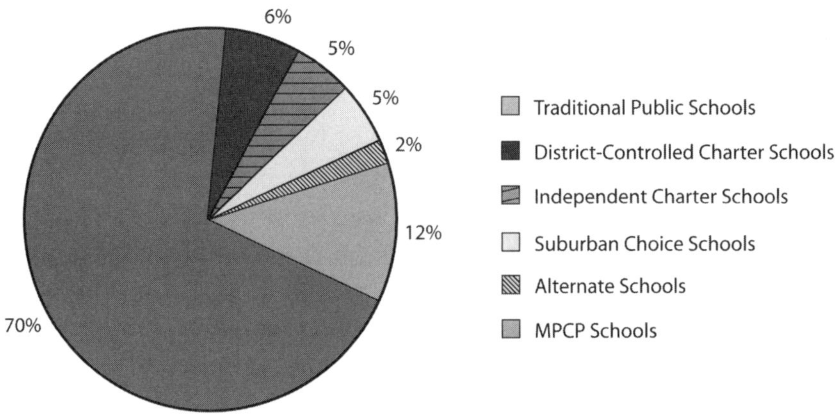

Fig. 3.3 Enrollment of Milwaukee Residents, by School Type, 2005
Note: Alternate schools are administered by the Milwaukee public schools but are exempt from many of its standard regulations. They serve specialized, mainly at-risk populations.
Sources: Milwaukee Public Schools for traditional school enrollment; Wisconsin Department of Public Instruction for charter school enrollment.

tance from the 10 percent participation rate in Milwaukee's voucher and charter schools six years previously. Clearly, the supply of choice-based schooling within a large central city can be highly elastic.

Conditions Facilitating Growth in Supply

Economic theory tells us that school supply can be expected to be highly elastic whenever the barriers to entry are minimal. We find evidence of this in the Milwaukee experience. Whenever the political, legal, and financial barriers were relaxed, the supply response was enhanced.

Legal and Political Environment

As in most parts of the United States, school choice in Wisconsin is a highly partisan political issue, with most Republicans and

Democrats firmly opposed to one another. As a result, shifts in the partisan composition of the legislature, or the gubernatorial chair, have translated into new laws, or interpretations of laws, that have had important consequences for choice school supply. At the local level, changes in the balance of power within the MPS's elected school board have also been of consequence. In 1999, a reform faction, with strong support from the mayor and the business community, won five seats, gaining control of the nine-member board. In subsequent years, majority control shifted back and forth between candidates endorsed by the school reform movement and those championed by teacher and other unions. In the last elections, in 2005, the reform faction regained control, but only by a one-vote margin. In 2006, the teachers union opposed the renewal of the school superintendent's contract and publicly announced that it plans to challenge reform members up for re-election in 2007. With power constantly in flux at both the state and local levels, many compromises have been struck and many policy adjustments have raised and lowered barriers to entry into the choice program.

Voucher Schools

In 1999, with the court decision finding the enlarged voucher program constitutional, important entry barriers fell. Religious schools could participate, up to around 15,000 students could be given vouchers, and the amount of the voucher was increased. As a result, supply changed almost overnight. The number of participating schools expanded immediately from twenty-three to eighty-six, and the number of participating students from 1,497 to 5,761. The major reason for the increment was the inclusion of schools with a religious affiliation since religious schools constituted nearly 90 percent of the private schools in Milwaukee (as well as elsewhere in the United States).

The extremely elastic supply response to the court decision was due mainly to two factors. First, sectarian schools had considerable available capacity. Many of the sectarian schools had been built by Catholic and Lutheran immigrants, who had left Milwaukee for the suburbs, leaving empty places behind. With an ample supply of under-utilized classrooms, these parochial schools immediately opened their doors to voucher recipients. Second, while waiting for the widely anticipated Wisconsin Supreme Court decision, voucher supporters prepared the schools and the students for a favorable outcome. Indeed, while the litigation was proceeding, many of the new voucher students from low-income families had already begun to attend private schools on privately-funded scholarships from Parents Advancing Values in Education (PAVE), an organization funded by community leaders and the Lynde and Harry Bradley Foundation. In a sense, much of both the demand and the supply were already in place; it was simply a matter of waiting for a court suit to be resolved.

Once the decision was handed down and the legal barriers to entry were reduced to a minimum—all that was required of private schools was that they apply for participation to the State Department of Education and that they possess a building that passed routine health and safety checks—the number of participating schools increased steadily. By 2003, the number had expanded to 107, with another rise to 117 by 2005. Enrollment also rose until it approached the maximum allowed by law.

Charter Schools

Changes in the supply of charter schools have also been strongly affected by political and legal developments. When the first Wisconsin school charter law was enacted in 1993, it had little impact. Originally, only two charter schools could be formed in any one district. Although this provision was later relaxed, MPS, the then sole authorizer for Milwaukee, had by 1997 granted only three charters to schools serving less than 200 students. But in that year new legislation gave chartering power to the city of Milwaukee and the University of Wisconsin-Milwaukee. Mayor John Norquist appointed Howard Fuller to head the city's Charter School Review Committee and encouraged him to begin granting charters to schools immediately. The first three schools approved by the city were up and running by the 1999 school year, and the first schools approved by UWM were operational by 2000.

Meanwhile, MPS, too, began approving new charter schools while at the same time converting traditional public schools to charter status, both to respond to the competition of the other authorizers and because pro-choice forces gained strength on the MPS school board. As part of a legislative compromise, MPS was given the authority to grant two different types of charters: independent and district-controlled.

District-controlled charter schools differ from the independent schools chartered by MPS in five main respects. First, teachers at district-controlled schools are represented in the collective bargaining process by the teachers union, while teachers at independent charters are not. Second, teachers at district-controlled schools receive all the benefits, including a handsome pension package that teachers at traditional public schools receive but teachers at independent charter schools do not. Third, the funding levels are different. Independent charters are given the same amount as independent charter schools authorized by the other two agencies, which in 2005 was $7,111 per pupil. District-controlled charters, however, receive the same amount as traditional public schools, which in 2005 was $9,024, plus whatever amount was necessary to sustain the teachers benefit package. Fourth, MPS assumes the responsibility for identifying an appropriate physical plant for any district-controlled charter school that was

Table 3.1 Number of Charter Schools by Authorizer and Source, 2005

	District-Controlled	*MPS Independent*	*UWM Schools*	*City of Milwaukee*	***Total***
Converted MPS Schools	14	2	0	0	**16**
Converted Voucher Schools	0	2	2	2	**6**
New Schools	7	10	5	2	**24**
Total	**21**	**14**	**7**	**4**	**46**

Source: School Choice Wisconsin, 2005b.

not a conversion from an existing public school. In all cases, district-controlled charter schools are placed in buildings formerly occupied by an MPS school. Meanwhile, independent charter schools are expected to find their own facility, which may or may not be a former public-school building. Fifth, district-controlled charter schools are required to pay to the central office a fee of $887 per pupil (in 2005) for a package of services. That same year independent charters paid a fee of $306 for a smaller set of services.

Charter schools may be new schools or schools that have been converted from some other legal status (Table 3.1). In 2005, two-thirds of the twenty-one district-controlled schools were conversions from traditional public school status. The remaining seven were started by former MPS employees. Of the fifteen independent schools chartered by MPS, two were converted from traditional public-school status, two had been voucher schools, and eleven were newly begun. Of the eleven charters authorized by the city and UWM, four were conversions from the voucher program, while the remainder consisted of start-up schools.

Whether or not conversions from traditional public school status add to school supply is a question that will be explored below. In 2005, of the sixteen schools converted from that status, fourteen were district-controlled while two were independent. Since 2000, there has been a steady increase in the number of conversion schools, though, as of 2006, a further increase in their number was not anticipated.

Financial Barriers

School formation and expansion are more attractive when government dollars are predictably available for both capital and operating costs. In the case of both the voucher and charter programs, government reimbursement takes place only after the educational service is ready to be provided and is often limited to cover tuition or school operating costs. As a result, new schools face, on their own, large start-up costs because they must acquire facilities, hire administrators and teachers long before the school door opens, and continue to pay employees while the school awaits reimbursement from the designated government agency.

Voucher Schools

Despite the financial obstacles, many new voucher schools have been able to form principally because the start-up costs are low given the limited government regulation to which they are subjected. In addition, private donations have helped with the start-ups as well as with the expansions. The financial barriers are lower for elementary schools, which receive the same voucher amount but need not offer a specialized curriculum or provide for athletic and other extra-curricular activities. As a result, most choice schools serve elementary school students. But for both elementary and high schools to grow in capacity, they need to mount fund-raising campaigns.

Many of Milwaukee's choice schools have sought support from PAVE, the organization that funded choice students during the years the MPCP was stalled in the courtroom. Once the favorable court decision was handed down, PAVE began to address supply-side issues. Indeed, it has been an important vehicle through which financial support has been channeled from a wide variety of local corporations and foundations, including the Bradley Foundation, which gave PAVE a $20 million matching grant.

Initially, PAVE played a passive role, reviewing applications and business plans submitted by those who wished to establish a school or expand existing operations. With experience, PAVE learned that a more pro-active strategy was required, simply because many educators had less well-formulated business plans than instructional visions. PAVE now works with the identified highest quality schools in MPCP, helping to develop a strategic plan, recruit volunteers, build connections to local foundations, cultivate relationships with banks and contractors, and conduct the fundraising necessary to create a successful campaign.

Charter schools

For charter schools, the financial constraints vary, depending on whether they are an independent or district-controlled charter. As mentioned before, the latter type of school is in the much more favorable position. It is provided with a physical plant by MPS; it receives a 20 percent higher reimbursement rate; its employees are paid by MPS, minimizing cash-flow problems; its staff recruitment is facilitated by the fact that its employees remain part of the collective bargaining agreement with all its salaries and benefits, including a substantial pension. Student recruitment is facilitated by the fact that students can matriculate directly into the charter school without first spending a year in a traditional MPS school, whereas independent charters cannot recruit a student until he or she has spent one year in an MPS school.

Not only do independent charter schools receive 20 percent less per pupil, but they face substantial capital costs as well. Years of planning may precede the approval of an application to the chartering agency; once approved, a building needs to be acquired and employees must be paid for substantial periods of time before the charter is reimbursed by the government. Apart from some federal funds, no government monies enter into a charter-school account until the month before school opens. Yet expenses do not wait for the first period bell to ring.

To cover some of these expenses, many independent charter schools have received a federally funded start-up grant worth anywhere between $10,000 and $150,000 over several years of planning and/or implementation. In 2002–03 alone, twenty-one of the thirty-one Milwaukee charter schools received grants totaling $2.35 million. These grants certainly help, but they are seldom adequate. To complete the task, the charter must locate financial backers in the private sector.

Conclusions

Many independent charter and voucher schools have overcome the financial barriers created by the legal arrangements in Milwaukee so that the supply of choice schools has expanded rapidly, once political and legal barriers were removed. Still, the challenges faced by many of these schools leaves the open question as to how much the availability of quality schools has expanded.

Growth in the Supply of Quality Schools

Measuring school quality is a challenging task, of course. Unless one can compare changes in the educational performance of students in choice schools with changes in the performance of a similar group of students in traditional public schools, one can not reach any definitive conclusions about their respective quality. The only studies that have done this were undertaken nearly a decade ago, and they examined only the initial, secular-only voucher program. While most of these studies found the voucher schools to be more effective,[7] the findings concerning this small program cannot necessarily be generalized to the much larger choice program now in place. But if definitive evidence is lacking, there is enough information from independent observers to make a reasonable, if preliminary, assessment.

Quality of Voucher Schools

The quality of voucher schools is highly variable. On the one side, one can certainly find areas of great strength, especially among the long-standing private schools that the program has helped to preserve. But, on the other side, a significant number of the newly established schools are quite problematic.

Signs of Program Strength

In the only recent systematic effort to determine the educational impact of the voucher program, Jay Greene[8] compared high school graduation rates for voucher students attending ten private high schools with rates at MPS high schools. To estimate graduation rates in 2003, the last year for which information was available, for each school, Greene compared the number of high school graduates with the number of high school freshman attending that school four years earlier, a method he had employed previously in a nationwide study of graduation rates.[9] He estimated that 64 percent of voucher students at the ten schools graduated from high school, as compared to only 36 percent of

7. For a summary of the findings see Jay Greene, Public Policy Forum, *MPS Outpacing New Charter Schools in Innovation, Achievement*, Research Brief, vol. 89, no. 9 (December 27, 2001).

8. Jay P. Greene, "Graduation Rates for Choice and Public School Students in Milwaukee," *School Choice Wisconsin*, September 28, 2004.

9. Jay P. Greene, "High School Graduation Rates in the United States" (Center for Civic Innovation at the Manhattan Institute and the Black Alliance for Educational Options, April 2002).

those who attended MPS high schools. To adjust for the possibility that voucher students are a select group, Greene also calculated graduation rates for six Milwaukee high schools that had selective admissions based upon prior academic achievement. The graduation rate for these six selective schools was only 41 percent, well below that of the voucher schools. As a further check on his methodology, he also estimated graduation rates using an alternative method proposed by the Harvard Civil Rights Project and the Urban Institute. Using their technique, voucher schools had a 67 percent graduate rate, selective MPS high schools had a 49 percent rate, and public schools, as a whole, had a graduate rate of 39 percent. Clearly, the secondary education provided to voucher students was superior to that available in MPS high schools.

Most of these secondary schools were long-standing parochial high schools that found the program critical to stabilizing their enrollments.[10] Indeed, reporters for the *Milwaukee Journal Sentinel*, after conducting a multi-part overview of the voucher program in the summer of 2005, concluded that "the principal effect of choice has been . . . to preserve the city's private schools, many of them Lutheran and Catholic."[11]

Data on private school enrollment justify this observation. Between 1967 and 1989, the number of students in Milwaukee who were attending private schools is estimated to have fallen from nearly 50,000 to just over 34,000. The slide continued during the 1990s and accelerated after 2000, when charter schools became available, so that today there are only around 22,000 students in

10. According to a researcher at the Public Policy Forum, the ten schools that had high school voucher students during this period were as follows: Divine Savior Holy Angels, Learning Enterprise, Marquette University High School, Messmer, Pius XI, Grandview, St. Joan Antida, Woodson Academy, Believers in Christ Academy, and Ceria M. Travis Academy. All but two of these schools have a religious affiliation.

11. Alan J. Borsuk and Sarah Carr, "Lessons from the Voucher Schools," *Milwaukee Journal Sentinel*, June 11, 2005.

private schools. Of that number, nearly two-thirds are recipients of school vouchers.[12] Were it not for vouchers, the decline would certainly have been more severe, especially after middle class families had the option of sending their children to tuition-free charter schools.

Most of the private schools participating in the voucher program have a religious affiliation. In 2005, more than 10,000 of the voucher students were attending religious institutions. In percentage terms, 39 percent were attending Catholic schools, 13 percent Lutheran schools, 22 percent other religious schools, 20 percent non-religious schools serving African-American students, and 6 percent "other" schools whose religious affiliation was not determined.[13]

Clearly, voucher revenues were helping parochial schools stabilize their operations and enhance their facilities. No less than sixty-two of the schools participating in MPCP began renovations, spending an estimated $80 million dollars on improvements in their physical plant since the choice program began.[14] Six either constructed a new building or added to the existing one, seventeen built new classrooms or laboratories, ten updated their electrical systems, eight added non-classroom space, and others painted and improved their heating and air-conditioning systems, while a scattering of others enhanced their property with new roofing, windows, handicapped accessibility, and other improvements.

Some of these expansions have been quite consequential. St. Marcus, a Lutheran elementary school, mounted a $5 million

12. Data made available by the Milwaukee Public Schools and the Wisconsin Department of Public Instruction to the *Milwaukee Journal Sentinel,* June 15, 2005.

13. Bob Veierstahler, "Schools Choice Students Attend," *Milwaukee Journal Sentinel,* June 12, 2005.

14. School Choice Wisconsin, *School Choice and Community Renewal,* September 2005a. School Choice Wisconsin, *Accurate Information about School Choice,* 2005b. http://www.SchoolChoiceWI.org.

campaign that was projected to increase capacity from 130 students to a projected 350 students. And Pius XI, a Catholic secondary school, began work on a new field house that contained classroom space as well. Meanwhile, the old gym was converted to a dramatic arts center.

Nor is it just traditional religious schools that have expanded in the wake of MPCP. In a heartwarming account, Sarah Carr, as part of the *Journal Sentinel's* overview, tells of a new school established by Cheryl Brown, both a trained nurse and a pastor of the Christian church, Believers in Christ, who started a school at her church, then pursued an education degree to strengthen her qualifications for the task at hand. The school now includes a high school, its leaders report that all its graduates have been accepted into college, and the church has purchased thirty-one acres on which it plans to build an urban education campus together with other facilities. "It was a mission from us in the beginning, an old time actual missionary assignment, a calling," Brown told the reporter.[15]

Another indication of enhanced quality has been the conversion of six schools from voucher to charter school status. (All six are secular schools, because religious schools cannot receive a government charter.) The incentives to switch are clear. Charters receive 20 percent more funding. State reimbursement can be obtained not just for low-income students but for any student in attendance, allowing the school to attract middle class families. Charter schools are also protected from the intense political controversy that continues to surround the voucher program even after its constitutional status was affirmed by the courts.

To achieve charter status, a school must convince one of Milwaukee's three chartering agencies that their offerings and oper-

15. Sarah Carr, "Mission Accomplished," *Milwaukee Journal Sentinel*, June 12, 2005.

ations justify government recognition, an achievement that requires an extended application. Charter school applicants must prepare a detailed educational and financial plan that the authorizing agency finds acceptable, a standard much higher than the minimum expectations for participation in MPCP.

Not surprisingly, the six schools that switched to charter status, who served 692 students the last year they were in the MPCP program, were among the strongest of MPCP's secular schools. Bruce Guadalupe, for example, had been one of the stars of the school voucher program in Milwaukee. Initially established within the basement of a Catholic church, it was on the verge of collapse in 1990 when the first, small, secular voucher program began. Indeed, it was featured in the local news media as the kind of disastrous school that the new voucher program was about to fund. But within a few years, it became the pride of the Latino community on Milwaukee's south side, winning business and governmental support for an expanding enrollment and the incorporation of other community programs serving all age groups. It raised the revenue to construct new, handsome buildings with modern equipment—even including child care services for employees. In 2000, MPS welcomed Bruce Guadalupe as one of its charter schools. Meanwhile, the no less respected Martha Collins school, Milwaukee College Preparatory School, which serves the African American community, converted to a UWM charter school even as it began a $4 million campaign that would allow itself to expand from 360 to 480 students. Officials at both Milwaukee College Preparatory School and Bruce Guadalupe said that the chance to grow, along with the certainty of having the cost of educating all their students covered by state payments, was crucial to their decision to convert to charter school status. Clearly, the voucher program has helped several schools move from marginal status to widely appreciated institutions that could win charter recognition.

Questionable Voucher Schools

While numerous voucher success stories can be told, not every school participating in MPCP has a quality reputation. On the contrary, even Milwaukee's strongest school-choice supporters have come to worry about the ease with which new schools, of problematic quality, have been able to attract students and secure state reimbursements under the voucher program. An official closely associated with the Catholic archdiocese of Milwaukee applauded recent efforts made to discourage weak schools from coming into being, noting that the effort was "about eight years too late" but one that was responding to a situation "we never saw . . . coming."[16] Similarly, choice supporter Robert Pavlik, director of the School Design and Development Center within the Marquette University Institute for the Transformation of Learning, concluded that, as of the summer of 2005, "there are about ten schools that ought to be closed immediately."[17] The reporters for the *Journal Sentinel* put the number somewhat higher. They reported that they were unable to visit nine of the 115 schools during their overview of the program, leaving them uneasy about what might have been taking place behind the closed doors. Inasmuch as schools often refuse access to outsiders, both to protect student privacy and to keep the school's focus on its educational objectives, one should not necessarily draw strong conclusions from this fact alone. But the reporters also asserted that "about 10 percent of the choice schools [implying ten to twelve schools] demonstrate alarming deficiencies" and named seven schools which left them with what they said were "major questions." At one school, there was only one teacher with two students, about to go to McDonalds. At others, supplies were

16. Alan J. Borsuk and Sarah Carr, "Questionable Scenes," *Milwaukee Journal Sentinel*, June 11, 2005b.

17. Alan J. Borsuk and Sarah Carr, 2005c.

limited, curriculum undefined, and teachers appeared unqualified.

Although the schools identified as deficient by the *Journal Sentinel* enrolled no more than 4.4 percent of all MPCP students, and some of these schools had just a few students, one, Harambee Community School, was particularly disappointing. It had been a major part of the original, secular voucher program and, in 2005, had 346 voucher students. In the cryptic words of the synopsis provided by reporters:

> Beset by internal fighting. Has had five principals in five years, high teacher turnover and financial problems, including former business manager being charged with stealing up to $750,000. Many of the teachers walked out briefly in a dispute with administrators. Some teachers do not have college degrees, unlike in the past.[18]

That a sizeable school that entered the voucher program as long ago as 1991 is judged to be so problematic in 2005 is certainly strong evidence that vouchers, by themselves, do not create strong schools.

Still another sign of the quality problem has been the school closure rate. Since MPCP began in the 1990–91 school year, fourteen of the participating schools had closed their operations by 2003, apparently because of financial problems or declining parental demand. Fortunately, these schools had, on average, many fewer voucher students than the average MPCP school. In the final year of their operations, they were serving only a total 642 voucher students, an average of less than forty-six students per school.

Interestingly enough, eight of these fourteen schools, like Harambee, had been among the twenty-three schools established un-

18. Alan J. Borsuk and Sarah Carr, "Questionable Scenes," *Milwaukee Journal Sentinel*, June 11, 2005b.

der the original MPCP program that was limited to secular schools. This translates into a 33 percent closure rate for the schools that helped inaugurate school choice in Milwaukee. It is ironic that the original, secular-only voucher program, the one that sparked the school choice movement nationwide, appears to have had serious weaknesses. Although a few of the early MPCP participants, most notably Bruce Guadalupe, capitalized on the new opportunity created by the program, too many of the secular organizations spawned by the program appear not to have deserved the official status given to them.

School choice supporters point out that closing weak schools is a viable strategy for enhancing the quality of urban education, a strategy that MPS needs to copy. Nonetheless, in 2005 choice supporters began taking steps to discourage the formation of new schools that do not seem up to the task at hand, urging the Wisconsin Department of Public Instruction to scrutinize the school's financial and educational plans before allowing a new voucher school to open. Their efforts seem to have had an effect. For the fall of 2006, over fifty additional school entrepreneurs had indicated an interest in joining the voucher program, but, only seventeen were approved by the department, with three applications still pending in spring 2006.

In sum, access to quality schooling under MPCP has been made possible largely because of the availability of strong parochial schools predating its inceptions. As established institutions, they were well placed to open their doors to low-income newcomers who were looking for alternatives to traditional public schools. In addition, a few secular schools, Bruce Guadalupe and Milwaukee College Preparatory School being the paramount examples, were led by educators capable of leveraging voucher dollars into quality education. But the number of weak and failing schools participating in the MPCP has been uncomfortably large.

One can only applaud any steps that are being taken to correct this situation.

Quality of Charter Schools

It has been the conventional wisdom that conversions from traditional public school to charter status are changes in name only, not mechanisms that provide leaders genuinely new opportunities to create higher quality institutions. Only a new school, with fresh leadership and innovative ideas, can truly break the deadlock in American education. That wisdom may be true elsewhere—and, in Milwaukee, it could still turn out to be correct over the long run. But, at least in the short run, conversion schools appear to be doing at least as well as other charter schools. Just exactly why charter conversion has proven to be an efficacious school choice strategy requires further consideration.

District-Controlled Schools

Converting a traditional public school to charter status has been advocated as a way of enhancing the quality of low-performing schools. Under the 2002 federal law, No Child Left Behind, for example, schools must be reconstituted, if student test scores fail to show adequate yearly progress toward state-determined proficiency standards for five consecutive years. One of the reconstitution options is for the school to be converted to charter status. Although few conversions have thus far taken place under NCLB, the thrust of the law is based on the assumption that conversion to charter status should be attempted when all else seems to have failed.

In Milwaukee, conversion of fourteen MPS schools from a traditional status to district-controlled charter status has come under completely different circumstances. It is a sign of success, not failure. MPS schools convert to charter status at the request of the school principal, with the support of at least half the teachers at the school. MPS is unlikely to grant the request unless it has confidence in the principal and the staff at the school. As a senior MPS administrator commented, when interviewed by one of us,

> When we first started chartering schools in Milwaukee, there was a general understanding that a [district-controlled] charter school would be an MPS school that had achieved a level of success that would allow it to use more flexibility and more autonomy effectively.

Similarly, MPS school superintendent William Andrekopoulos commented to a newspaper reporter that converted schools "were probably doing well before they became charter schools,"[19] a conclusion also reached by the Public Policy Forum (2001), a Milwaukee-based think-tank that studies school choice.[20]

Principals and teachers seek charter status in order to gain exemption from various school regulations and certain provisions of the teacher union contract. For example, charter schools, though still district-controlled, may select new teachers, not simply on the basis of seniority, but by a site-based selection committee (a practice that MPS now appears to be instituting system wide). Although this committee must still conform to certain union guidelines (such as interviewing teachers with greater seniority first), it still has more autonomy in the hiring process than do traditional public schools. Also, the district-controlled charters have greater capacity to release unsatisfactory teachers that are either not yet tenured or on probation. Charter schools can also secure "Memorandums of Understanding (MOUs)" for specific programs, such as the one at Juneau High School, which has a special January term. The principal there told our interviewer

19. Sarah Carr, "Number of Milwaukee-area Students in Charter Schools Increases," *Milwaukee Journal Sentinel*, December 30, 2002, 1A.

20. Jay Greene, Public Policy Forum, *MPS Outpacing New Charter Schools in Innovation, Achievement*, Research Brief, vol. 89, no. 9 (December 27, 2001).

that "it is easy to get the MOU approved by the union because in most cases we have been able to get 50 to 60 percent of the staff to buy in, and when we present that data to the union and the district, it's easy to get the MOU." Similarly, the principal at Fritsche Middle School told us that "if you have a charter, the union is more flexible with you."

That said, union regulations still bind district-controlled charter schools. Some principals complained to us that the union, despite certain concessions, still hinders schools from compensating teachers according to ability and subject need as well as from using adequate authority to recruit the most effective teachers. In an anonymous comment, one admitted:

> I have to be honest with you. I don't really like [the terms of our status as a district-controlled charter]. We need to have the ability to hire and fire teachers. Even with . . . site-based hiring, HR [Human Resources] sometimes sends people over here based on the contract. We can't always find the people that believe the most in our program.

But despite these limitations on their autonomy, district-controlled charter schools enjoy many advantages *vis a vis* the independents.

Independent Charters

Independent charters stand midway between the district-controlled charters and the schools operating within the MPCP framework. As compared to the latter, independent charters have decisive advantages, as is evidenced by the fact that six voucher schools have converted to charter status (while none have gone in the other direction). Although independent charters must go through a more rigorous application stage than that required of MPCP schools, their reimbursement rate is 20 percent larger, they can be reimbursed for any type of student, not just those coming from low-income families, they have the more prestigious status of a governmentally chartered school, and they escape the political controversy that still surrounds MPCP.

At the same time, independent charters face many challenges district-controlled charters escape. They must locate their own physical plant, they incur many start-up costs, they have a lower reimbursement rate, and they cannot recruit MPS employees unless those employees are willing to forgo a substantial benefits package. Although private resources have helped independent charters overcome some of the financial challenges, the task of raising the money can, as one principal admitted, distract them from the recruitment of talented teachers and preparation for the initial school year. Until 2005, no student could enter directly into an independent charter school; they had to first attend for one year a traditional public school. In other words, charters had to be constantly addressing the transfer-student problem. The recent repeal of this provision has certainly been a positive step forward.

All of these challenges—and others—were evident in the early years of Milwaukee's charter program. "The first year we just muddled through," said one principal, adding that "everybody's first year is really tough." Another principal admitted that she came in "not knowing anything about running schools" and, as a result often felt "a lot of frustration" because she was always struggling just "to get all the administrative stuff done." Commenting from the vantage point of a conversion school, one principal expressed sympathy with start-ups chartered by MPS: The new schools "would probably have a harder time because they won't know all the bureaucracy and they won't understand many times how to get things done at Central Office." The challenges were so great for three of the twenty-eight independent charter schools that they closed. Two of those charters were authorized by the city, which initially had a more lax set of authorizing procedures.

With the passage of time, however, all authorizing agencies took increasing care before granting a charter.

As policy analyst Bryan Hassel has observed, "Charter schools, in addition to being educational institutions, have to succeed as small businesses; balancing their budgets, negotiating leases, financing packages and contracts, and making payroll. Individuals and small teams . . . are apt to possess some but not all of these skills and backgrounds."[21] Those abilities, which on their own are difficult to muster in a start-up team, must be complemented by expertise in curriculum design, facility maintenance, management, and community relations. In addition, independent charter starters must plan for providing transportation, food service, and appropriate zoning. Altogether, they represent a daunting, if not insurmountable, undertaking for many prospective educators. Building a quality charter school takes time.

Conclusions: Systemic Impact and Recommendations

While the overall supply of choice schools in Milwaukee has proven to be considerably more elastic than the supply of quality schools, the rapid increase in the percentage of students exploring choice options may still have had a broad, systemic impact on schools in Milwaukee. With many choices available, public schools are under pressure to respond to the competition.

Impacts on Traditional Public Schools

Since 1999, MPS schools have suffered a more than 5 percent enrollment loss, from around 101,000 students to 95,600 in 2005—even when one considers district-controlled charters to be part

21. Bryan C. Hassel, "Friendly Competition," *Education Next* 3, no.1 (Winter 2003).

of the MPS system. Enrollment declines forced closures of four traditional public schools in 2005. To forestall a further slide, MPS has introduced a wide range of policies designed to make traditional public schools in the city more attractive to parents and students. Here are just some of the more important actions that have taken place:

1. In 2001, the school board appointed as its superintendent someone who had been a renegade principal, one of the first to convert his school from traditional to charter status. In 2005, the board renewed his contract for another four years, if only by a divided vote.
2. In 2001, the school board mandated that more than 70 percent of the operating budget in the district "follow the student" to the school they entered. In other words, each MPS school's budget is partly determined by its enrollment, which gives principals incentives to take steps to create as attractive an educational setting as possible.
3. After learning from a system-wide survey of parents that they prefer K–8 schools to K–5 schools, the number of K–8 schools has increased in the last few years from eighteen to fifty-six.
4. After learning from the survey of parents that they wish to have before-and-after school day programs as well as full-day kindergarten beginning at age four, elementary schools have been given the opportunity to introduce these programs.
5. With the support of a number of private foundations, small schools are being formed within large high schools.
6. Outreach and advertising have been increased. For example, the district spent over $103,000 in TV, radio, and billboard ads during the two-month period from January to March of 2004. As MPS's director of student services put it in one of our interviews: "We were advertising before the choice pro-

gram began, but it has increased—competition tends to do that to you." Individual schools are also conducting their own advertising campaigns.

While many signs are promising, we cannot be certain that the increased competition has translated into higher levels of student achievement. Still, Milwaukee public school student performance on the Wisconsin-mandated test has improved over the past decade. Between 1997 and 2005, the percentage of third-graders scoring at or above proficiency levels in reading increased from 50 percent to 71 percent. And, with just two exceptions, average test-score performance in all grades increased significantly in fourth, eighth, and tenth grades in reading, language arts, math, science, and social studies. While these improvements do not appear to exceed those achieved in the state as whole, more rigorous research found larger gains in those public schools that were most directly impacted by the voucher program than in schools less directly affected.[22] Still, that study was conducted only shortly after the expanded program was put into place and was unable to track progress by individual students. We must wait for still more refined analyses over a longer period of time before coming to definite conclusions.

In this regard, it is unfortunate that the degree of competition may have reached a new ceiling. The voucher program is about as large as the law allows, though voucher proponents were making special efforts in the Wisconsin state legislature to allow more students to participate in the voucher program. Meanwhile, there is little evidence that a spate of new charter schools will soon be established. Even as a strong supporter of choice, the current MPS school superintendent is not expecting much growth in the coming years. Once again, the Milwaukee experience underlines the

22. Caroline M. Hoxby, "Rising Tide: New Evidence on Competition and the Public Schools," *Education Next* 1, no. 4 (Winter 2001): 68–75.

critical importance of the political and legal situation surrounding school choice programs.

Recommendations

If the final word on Milwaukee remains to be written, one can still draw preliminary conclusions about the promises and pitfalls of its complex system of school choice innovation. On the positive side, a choice system that engages the private sector, especially if it includes schools with a religious affiliation, can preserve—and enhance—the contributions these schools have long made to American education at a time when their future within central cities is in jeopardy. And a policy of converting successful public schools to charter status can give talented principals and staff the flexibility they need to raise their schools to still higher levels of performance. The possibility of moving from voucher to charter status can give greater permanence to newly formed but promising secular schools.

On the negative side, problematic schools will form as well. A choice program can reduce their number, if not eliminate them altogether, if it takes such steps as the following:

1. Establish reasonable educational, financial, and physical-plant requirements before allowing a school to participate in a choice program.
2. Establish a level financial playing field by providing reimbursements equivalent to the amount received by traditional public schools operating within the community. With adequate resources, entrepreneurs who have the capability of establishing quality schools will be more likely to participate.
3. Give principals at successful public schools incentives to convert their school to charter status. In general, charter status should be a reward for success, not a punishment for failure.

4. Provide vouchers to students regardless of family income. Any school-choice program that limits support to those of low-income creates socially-segregated institutions.
5. Allow direct entry to schools of choice without first requiring attendance at a traditional public school. Since transfers among schools are often educationally costly, they should not be mandated.
6. Provide funding for advance planning and capital costs as well as arrange for a procedure to help choice schools with their initial cash flow problems.
7. Create an accountability system that allows for early identification of low-performing schools.
8. Build a political base of support that can sustain an increasingly competitive system over the long run.

4. Authorizing: The Missing Link

Chester E. Finn Jr.
and **Paul T. Hill**

Authorizers, AKA sponsors, were the most neglected part of the charter school phenomenon in the early days. Though it would be an exaggeration to say that these new schools were expected to come into existence via immaculate conception, their parentage received scant attention. In *Charter Schools in Action,* the 2000 book by Manno, Finn and Vanourek that was as careful a look at the charter world as any at the time, "sponsors" accounted for no more than half a dozen paragraphs that rather ambiguously depicted them as second party to the "contract" by which a charter operator was able to launch a school.

Even such primal charter-school theorists as the late Ray Budde and Albert Shanker paid little attention to the subject of sponsorship. They focused more on innovative schools than novel governance arrangements. Ted Kolderie recalls that Budde's original "proposal was actually for a restructuring of the district: for moving from 'a four-level line and staff organization' to 'a two-level form in which groups of teachers would receive educational charters directly from the school board.'" But the school board was still the school board and would function accordingly.

Though it would in fact be issuing an "educational charter," nobody spent a lot of time or thought on how its role might need to change as it shifted from bureaucratic to contractual governance. The emphasis was on the freedom those on the receiving end would enjoy and the fresh educational opportunities it would afford.

With time, Budde's own thinking evolved. By 1996, he could see in the early charter movement "more powerful dynamics at work in creating a whole new school than in simply restructuring a department or starting a new program." And Ted Kolderie was picturing wide consequences from ending the "exclusive franchise" of district-wide systems to deliver public education. Yet the act of authorizing, the nature of authorizers and the hallmarks of doing this well captured scant interest until recently, even from those immersed to their eyebrows in the charter pond. Nearly all of their attention focused on schools and operators, not on the public bodies that license them to operate.

In retrospect, this is understandable. People who were eager to start their own schools wanted and needed permission to proceed but had no interest in becoming entangled with government overseers, especially if these were local school boards, which were prone reflexively to impose new rules whenever problems arose. Early in the charter movement, school boards also saw charter schools as something inflicted upon them by the state. These breakaway schools could take money previously controlled by districts and need not respond to every change in district policy—an alarming development from the boards' perspective. Board members were reinforced in this by denizens of their district central offices, who also felt a loss of control and feared that, despite their limited leverage over charter schools, they would be blamed for failures.

With the benefit of hindsight, we can see that few legislators or governors thought deeply about this new form of public-education governance. Perhaps picturing charter schools as akin to "magnet" or "alternative" schools, most state policymakers simply assumed that local districts would add sponsorship to their brimming plates. The many vested interests of public education encouraged this assumption, by doing their utmost in the political horse-trading around charter laws to ensure that *only* local boards would have this authority. Indeed, confining sponsorship to local school districts would prove to be a powerful inhibitor of the charter movement—which is precisely why the teachers' unions, school board associations and superintendents' groups wanted it that way.

Exceptions were made, however, and not surprisingly the first people to pay close attention to authorization itself were the heads of a few special agencies, boards and units whose only mission was to charter schools. The Massachusetts charter law established a dedicated chartering office under the state secretary of education and separate from the education department. California's and Colorado's laws allowed would-be school operators who were turned down by their local districts to appeal to the state board of education, which established a special staff to handle these appeals. The District of Columbia law set up a separate dedicated chartering authority, which proved to be a more diligent reviewer of applications and overseer of schools than the D.C. school board (which also had sponsorship powers). Arizona created a statewide charter board whose authority in this area paralleled that of the state board of education. Michigan's charter law allowed state universities to authorize charter schools, and one campus, Central Michigan University, established a new unit solely to manage that work.

These special-purpose chartering units had a strong interest in the success of the schools that they authorized. Their own reputations and the political futures of their leaders depended on those schools' performance. Central Michigan University quickly learned this lesson the hard way, when a scathing report accused it of lax oversight of the schools it had chartered. Specialized agencies, however, did not guarantee thoughtful chartering. For every example of one that took its sponsorship duties seriously, there is at least one offsetting instance of a special agency that simply authorized all comers and left their oversight to the market. Examples include the Texas and Ohio Departments of Education and local education service centers in many states. Still, the handful of diligent authorizers demonstrated the principle: that thoughtful oversight was possible and could pay off both in fostering superior school performance and in minimizing meltdowns at the hands of school operators who never should have been counted upon to succeed in this complex endeavor.

Making Sense of Authorizing

Licensure and contracting are decent analogies for the role of the authorizer. The former implies an agent of the state giving permission to a private vendor, person or organization to engage in a certain line of work or operate a particular kind of shop or agency. Americans are accustomed to drivers' licenses, liquor licenses, plumbers' licenses, elevator licenses, licenses to operate nursing homes, hospitals, even private schools. (Most states also have established procedures for licensing private schools to operate. In Pennsylvania, for example, that license must be renewed annually.) Under this arrangement, a state licensing agency confers certain rights and authorities on the licensee, normally for a limited period of time (after which the license must be renewed) and usually after checking to see if the licensee meets certain requirements or qualifications. It's a familiar governmental activity, albeit very different from operating a public school system.

Contracting is somewhat different. Contracting is how a public body charged with supplying specific goods or services can arrange with private providers to supply them. Whereas licensure normally happens at the initiative of the licensee, government contracting usually starts with the public agency seeking for something to be done but, instead of doing it directly (with state employees, for example), arranging for it to be provided by other private (or sometimes public) entities. Thus, the Air Force does not build planes; it contracts with Boeing or Lockheed. The highway department does not actually employ the people who pour asphalt; it gets roads built by contracting with private firms. Sometimes this is called outsourcing. Under the theory of "reinventing government" popularized in the early 90s by David Osborne and Ted Gaebler, government should "steer, not row" and should get more of its work done via outsourcing, using competitive processes to achieve greater efficiency and quality than it could do directly.

American public education has long contracted for sundry goods and services, from cafeteria food and school buses to computers and textbooks. Certain professional services are also routinely obtained via contract, such as school doctors, psychologists, social workers, speech therapists and other specialists. In recent years, some school systems have contracted with private bodies to run entire schools; sometimes these are "alternative" schools for troubled youths; sometimes (e.g. Philadelphia, Baltimore) they outsource the management of poorly functioning schools to private firms that undertake to turn them around. There is no bright line of distinction between this practice and the authorizing of charter schools. There may, indeed, be a continuum, and the district's role as contractor for whole-school operations may closely parallel that of charter-school authorizer.

Thus the work of authorizing (or sponsoring) schools actually has multiple precedents in American government, even in K–12 education, which in turn may help explain why so little attention was paid to this role for so long in the charter-school context.

With one prominent exception: in every state considering passage of a charter law, there was debate and usually conflict about who would be allowed to authorize such schools. This had mainly to do with control and politics, of course. In general, the public-school establishment sought to confine charter authorizing to districts while most charter advocates sought to confer sponsorship powers on other entities believed to be more sympathetic to the actual creation of independent charter schools—and to devise multiple paths to sponsorship so that energized school operators turned down by one authorizer could seek approval by another. Where charter advocates failed to persuade lawmakers to entrust these more sympathetic entities with actual sponsorship powers, they tried, sometimes successfully, to create appellate arrangements such that a statewide body could reverse negative decisions by local school boards. (In addition to Colorado and California, "appeals" arrangements were added later in Florida and Pennsylvania.)

Putting it differently: people didn't pay much heed to the role of the authorizer or how to get it right and do it well, but they paid ample attention to the power of authorizers to license competitors to the traditional system and, predictably, the traditional system did its utmost to restrict that power to itself.

Which is not to say the system was eager to shoulder this role, much less that it was capable of doing a good job. Once people started seeking charters and running actual schools, it became clear that, much as they wanted to retain this monopoly for themselves, local districts, by and large, knew neither how to appraise potential schools and would-be operators nor how to monitor the performance of existing schools. Somehow, districts were equipped to manage separate parts of schools—teacher hiring, bus routes, textbook purchasing, special ed programs etc.—but knew little to nothing about schools as organizations.

How did it happen that school districts, whose sole job seems to be to provide schools, became focused instead on parts of schools and services ancillary to schools? Part of the answer can be found above them in the governmental food chain. Desegregation lawsuits and Office for Civil Rights enforcement actions led districts to consider schools as bins into which the right mixtures of children and programs were to be put. Federal categorical programs required school districts to focus on whether particular streams of funds were being administered properly, or whether the proper special services were going to eligible kids (and only to those youngsters). Legislatures proliferated school boards' duties, as they resolved emergent problems simply by requiring local districts and their boards to address them. Teachers' unions, empowered by collective bargaining laws, won contracts that took away principals' authority and made school staffing dependent on senior teachers' preferences. The result was that school boards had strong incentives to manage categorical programs, compliance with court orders, teacher contracts, and the demands of special education parents—and scant incentive to oversee entire individual schools, over which they had no real leverage.

Changing Times

The era of standards-based reform dawned about the same time as the charter-school era. Each would prove a tough test of districts' competence in looking holistically at schools, judging them by results and knowing how to diagnose and remedy performance shortcomings in these complex organizations. In general, districts shirked these challenges, avoiding chartering except in rare cases and reporting test results but seldom acting strongly to change or replace low performing schools.

A handful of districts, however, glimpsed the power of charters as a promising way of doing business. Chicago, Philadelphia,

San Diego, Cincinnati (briefly), recently New York City are prominent in that handful—school systems that came to see chartering as one way to provide educational options in neighborhoods where the regular public schools were intractably bad and their own internal rules and contracts made it ridiculously hard to turn such schools around. They, too, created specialized oversight units, which had a strong incentive both to give schools the freedom necessary for innovation and to oversee them carefully enough to prevent scandalous failures.

To date, though, they're the exception. Even in the face of NCLB requirements that districts consider chartering as a means to intervene in failing schools and to create viable alternatives for children trapped in such schools, few districts are paying attention. Moreover, even those that have chartered some schools tend to remain in the passive-aggressive mode, keen to show that, if they give charter schools enough rope, they'll hang themselves and then legislators will reconsider this whole charter folly.

Politically, too, most districts are still hostile, often aggressively so. In many a statehouse, board members and administrators team up with the teacher unions to restrict, cap, regulate, de-fund or roll back the charter movement—and to elect candidates who share those goals. Although districts are the most numerous authorizers—a recent survey by the National Charter School Research Center finds that they comprise 85 percent of all active sponsors—many are at best reluctant and semi-competent in this role, and at worst antagonistic and truly inept.

Besides the technical challenge of authorizing schools, districts run political risks if they encourage charters. Teachers' unions generally oppose such schools, which threaten their hegemony and create jobs for teachers who are not part of the district-wide bargaining unit. In Ohio, for example, to the extent that any districts are functioning as sponsors, it's extremely rare and profoundly opposed by the teachers union. Cincinnati's Steve

Adamowski, the one Buckeye superintendent who tried creatively to use charters to expand his district's portfolio of diverse, high performing schools, soon lost his job after the union rallied to oppose him. Former San Diego superintendent Alan Bersin's predilection to make constructive use of the chartering option was also one of the ways that he made himself anathema to the city's teacher union, which strove mightily, and in time successfully, to dislodge him via school board elections.

A Tractable Problem

A handful of authorizers have taken the job seriously and are trying to figure out how this novel role can be played effectively. As they succeed they will pave the way for willing school districts and other authorizers to benefit from their experience. The National Association of Charter School Authorizers (NACSA) has developed a set of "principles and standards for quality charter school authorizing" (see http://www.charterauthorizers.org/files/nacsa/BECSA/Quality.pdf) and is working to assemble examples of thoughtful problem solving. Via conferences and publications, NACSA is also trying to convince school district leaders and other sponsors both that good charter authorizing is not rocket science and that it can pay off.[1]

NACSA head Greg Richmond was formerly head of the much-admired Chicago charter school office. His fledgling orga-

1. A sampling of recent NACSA publications includes: *Principles and Standards for Quality Charter School Authorizing*; *A Reference Guide to Special Education Law for Charter School Authorizers*; *Charter School Accountability Action Guide*; *Charter School Accountability: A Guide to Issues and Options for Charter Authorizers*; *Charter Schools and the Education of Students with Disabilities*; *Charting a Clear Course: A Resource Guide for Building Successful Partnerships Between Charter Schools & School Management Organizations*; *Guidelines for Ensuring the Quality of a National Design-Based Assistance Provider*; and *Measuring Up: How Chicago's Charter Schools Make Their Missions Count.*

nization is underwritten by many of the same foundations that have supported development of new charter schools, including Walton, Gates, Pisces, and Fordham. Despite its ambitions, however, NACSA reaches only a small fraction of the school districts and other agencies that could, under state law, serve as school authorizers. It claims ninety-six members in twenty-seven states, while some 854 entities are currently sponsoring charter schools and as many as 10,000 entities (in forty-three states) are empowered to do so. Among today's active authorizers are found 732 local school boards or districts, forty-four county boards and education service centers, thirty-seven institutions of higher education, twenty-two state agencies, seventeen non-profit groups and two city governments.

Belatedly, too, bits of research are being done on the role and performance of charter authorizers.[2] Yet this remains an underdeveloped scholarly field that basically lacks theory, data, even a solid database. The upshot is that there's little to counter one's natural tendency to judge a sponsor as one judges a school system or school board. Yet that's shortsighted and wrong—serving to cram charters back into the usual mold rather than creating the new model that their governance cries for.

The authorizing problem could be more readily solved if both sponsors and school operators viewed chartering as a risk-sharing arrangement between two parties that want to attain the same objective. It is, in effect, a way to attain a public purpose via a structured collaboration between government and private actors.

2. See, for example, Rebecca Gau, *Apples, Oranges, Plums and Pears: Charter School Authorizer Trends and Types* (Washington DC: Thomas B. Fordham Institute, 2006), and Bryan C. Hassel and Meagan Batdorff, *High Stakes: Findings from a National Study of Life-or-Death Decisions by Charter School Authorizers* (Chapel Hill: Public Impact, February 2004). See also Louann Bierlein and Rebecca Gau, *Charter School Authorizing, Are States making the Grade?* (Washington DC: Thomas B. Fordham Institute, 2003), and Paul T. Hill and Robin J. Lake, *Charter Schools and Accountability in Public Education* (Washington DC: Brookings Institution Press, 2002).

Table 4.1 A Risk-Sharing Scheme for Authorizers and Charter Schools

	Consequences (compensation owed if one party defaults)	
Risk	*Borne by charter authorizer*	*Borne by school operator*
Low enrollment		•
Inability to find teachers		•
Late or partial payments to school	•	
School inability to meet financial obligations		•
School inability to secure a private building		•
District's inability to provide a promised building	•	
Disruption, conflict within the school		•
Changes in district attendance boundaries	•	
Failure to reach enrollment goals for disadvantaged		•
Frequent turnover of teaching staff		•
Change in demographics, needs of students enrolled	•	
New compliance requirements	•	
Unavailability of promised district services	•	
Low student performance		•
Loss of promised state or federal funds	•	
Shortfall in private fund raising		•

Which is no simple feat. Starting and running a new school, or authorizing someone else to do so, is inherently risky. No one can be sure in advance whether a school will attract the students and teachers it needs to survive, whether a promising instructional method will actually work, or whether other events (from state budget cuts to fires, floods, and school-bus accidents) will make it impossible for one of the parties to meet its obligations. Prior to launching a new charter school, smart authorizers and operators both identify the major risks and agree in advance on who is responsible for what. Neither side should be in a position where it has no recourse if the other fails to deliver. Table 4.1 presents a risk allocation scheme that could make chartering a realistic contract between public agencies and individual school operators. The asterisks indicate the most sensible assignments of risk.

To our knowledge, no school charter has ever been constructed upon such an agreement. Instead, authorizers and operators typically hope things will work out and would just as soon avoid hard discussions about who is responsible for what and how. If one side fails to deliver as expected or uncontrollable events occur, this type of agreement can help restore the relationship to working order—or terminate it altogether.

Even as little is done to develop a sound theory of charter sponsorship, a tight but mutually respectful contract between authorizer and operator, or a framework of shared and apportioned responsibility for doing it well, the sponsorship world is evolving at a rapid clip. The most interesting development is the decision by a few states to entrust with authorizer powers entities that are neither local school districts nor creatures of the regular K–12 system. State universities came first, with Michigan, Minnesota, New York and Ohio leading the way. The Indiana legislature empowered the mayor of Indianapolis to function in this capacity, and Wisconsin conferred sponsorship powers on the Milwaukee city council. And in both Minnesota and Ohio, non-profit organizations that gain approval from the state department of education may function as charter-school sponsors.

This broadening of the definition of eligible authorizers is an interesting and potentially momentous development. It signals to districts that they can expect other bodies, including some that they do not control and may not even be able to influence, to authorize competing schools to operate within and sometimes across their boundaries. Well aware of this, districts commonly strive to contain and control this phenomenon, such as by trying to drive state universities out of sponsorship by threatening not to hire their graduates (such is the case in Michigan and Toledo, Ohio). It doesn't take much, usually, to convince risk-averse college presidents that a strong record of producing employed and contented alumni/ae is more important than a few irksome charter schools that view the university as their parent.

Yet if the charter movement survives and is allowed to grow, the effort to expand the sponsorship rolls will grow with it. Such expansion signals that state policymakers are wresting monopoly control from school districts and, to some extent, from the state public-education bureaucracy, and are seeking more creative or trustworthy agents to accomplish this vital public purpose. They are, in fact, withdrawing the "exclusive franchise." At the same time, they must preserve some sort of "chain of command" in order to satisfy state constitutional provisions governing public education. In Ohio and Minnesota, the non-profit authorizers are, in effect, licensed by and accountable to the state department of education. It remains to be seen whether states will come to trust the boards of major non-profits as they do the regents of their colleges and universities—to operate in the public interest with minimal government oversight. Because school districts are no longer the only imaginable sponsors of charter schools, the extent to which they remain dominant in this arena will depend on how seriously they take and how successfully they perform the role of authorizer. This, of course, means suppressing their natural bias in favor of traditional district-run public schools. It's an inherent dilemma for them, so long as they're also running their own schools, because they are, in effect, licensing their own competition—an inherently unstable situation.

This future also depends, of course, on how well non-district authorizers do at performing the key functions of sponsorship and demonstrating that they might be better at it than school boards and district offices. In doing so, they face a host of challenges—all of them exacerbated by the lean rations and adverse climate surrounding the wider charter movement. It's tough even to get authorizers funded and staffed, and we're beginning to see that, important as it is to have multiple authorizers in a state, a sponsorship "marketplace" brings its own perversities. (For example, what would induce a school operator to choose a relatively high-priced and fussy-about-results sponsor when the options include laissez-faire authorizers that charge lower fees?) Insofar as sponsors depend on their schools for revenue, they have a financial incentive to authorize lots of (big) schools—and not to close any down.

It is also wise to bring a healthy Madisonian skepticism to new governance schemes. Even when it's clear the old one is not working well—and that's plainly true of district-run public schooling, especially in urban America—we cannot take for granted that sheer innovation will yield improvement. All the issues that the founders struggled with in Philadelphia (e.g. separation of powers, minority rights, pluralism versus uniformity) arise in education governance, too, and will have to be worked through—probably with missteps—as the charter movement evolves.

What Is Good Authorizing?

What does it mean to do well in the authorizer's role? It starts with ensuring that the schools one sponsors comply with applicable laws about admissions, use of funds, civil rights, and public reporting. But compliance is just the tip of the sponsorship iceberg. Doing this job well also means exercising imaginative and discerning judgment about which aspiring school operators are likely to succeed in providing quality instruction, managing their business affairs and building a well-functioning and sustainable organization. It means knowing when and how to blow the whistle on a malfunctioning school and how to strike a defensible balance between providing it with needed technical assistance and objectively appraising its strengths and weaknesses on behalf of the public interest. Above all, in this era of standards-based reform and No Child Left Behind, it means holding the school to account for its results, both those built into statewide academic standards and those school-specific education goals and performance measures that distinguish one charter school from the next. Some authorizers go further, moving from quality control of individual schools to broader strategies meant to advance the charter movement itself and increase the supply and diversity of sound education options available in a community or region.

Table 4.2 summarizes what good authorizing entails under three headings, distinguishing among compliance-, quality-, and promotion-focused authorizing. Specific authorizer actions are listed below each heading. The actions are listed in temporal order, so that the ones appearing at the top of the table are naturally done before those appearing lower, and the actions on the same row happen at about the same time. The point is not to classify a particular authorizer under one or another heading—though many can be—but to recognize that good authorizing entails complex actions of three quite different sorts.

Are all of these functions compatible? They certainly can be, though many extant sponsors may gaze in puzzlement upon some of them. The legal compliance functions are necessary but manifestly insufficient. A compliance-focused authorizer could overlook many opportunities to charter good schools while also allowing weak but obedient schools to obtain and keep charters. There are, moreover, examples of authorizers that take the compliance functions seriously but also promote quality schools. Central Michigan University not only demands that all charter schools file every report required by the state; it also gives schools the report formats and basic data they need to complete those documents. Taking compliance seriously does not prevent Central Michigan University from promoting school quality and working proactively to find and promote promising charter providers.

Table 4.2 Elements of Good Authorizing

Compliance-Focused	*Quality-Focused*	*Promotion-Focused*
		Ensuring that all potentially qualified applicants know they can apply for charters
	Creating clarity about the standards to be used in judging proposals	
	Developing the capacity to tell the difference between groups that have vs lack clear ideas about instruction and capacity for financial management	
Making sure charter operators understand their legal obligations		Helping promising applicants improve their proposals
	Creating contracts that spell out the respective duties and rights of both charter school and authorizer	
	Ensuring that existing schools are not harmed by the authorizer's failure to keep its own promises	
Monitoring school admissions and finances for compliance with the law	Monitoring leading indicators of school performance, in order to intervene in a failing school before students lose a whole year's instruction	
	Creating clear criteria for closing failed schools and re-chartering good schools when charter terms expire	
	Planning for the possibility that some schools will fail, to ensure that children can transfer to sounder schools	
		Encouraging expansion or replication of high performing charter schools

Some might claim that the promotional activities in the right-hand column surely conflict with compliance and quality control. Yes, it's possible for an entrepreneurial authorizer to neglect the quality control functions, encouraging marginal applicants to apply and taking risks by approving underdeveloped proposals. Some Arizona and California school districts have apparently followed this approach—even approving schools to operate in localities other than their own—in order to skim the oversight fees and additional enrollment counts that state law makes available to sponsors.

Yet the Chicago school district and the D.C. Charter Board offer proof that authorizing can be both ambitious and quality-focused. Both encourage promising applications via public information sessions and workshops, and both suggest ways whereby interesting applicants can gain capacities missing from their original proposals. Chicago even encourages competent charter operators to take on additional challenges—including opening more campuses. However, Chicago has also shown its willingness to close bad charter schools and withdraw a charter before a school opens if the school's finances or academic program seem near collapse. The independent D.C. chartering authority has been tougher on the schools it approves than the District's board of education, which has apparently granted charters to political cronies and allowed abusive situations to continue.

It would be understandable if special chartering authorities like universities opted to limit themselves to the compliance and quality control functions. They risk some institutional prestige if the schools they sponsor get into legal or financial trouble or prove ineffective. Moreover, these authorizers have no responsibility for the overall quality of public schools in city or state. It is reasonable for them to set high standards for the schools they charter, even if these standards are higher than surrounding public schools can meet.

Districts face the toughest challenges. Like special chartering agencies, they must be concerned with compliance and school quality. But they are also responsible for the education of all the children in an area. They surely couldn't justify setting lower standards for charters than for other public schools, but could they reasonably set *higher* standards for charters? Does it make sense for them to turn down a charter application that would lead to a school only slightly better than the district-run schools available, or to close a struggling charter while lower-performing district schools stay open? It is hard to see how districts can do these things, given their responsibilities for the education of all children in their areas. Nonetheless, many refuse to consider promising charter proposals and take action against charter schools even while doing nothing about worse district-run schools.

The three strands of quality authorizing also call upon sponsors to develop multiple forms of expertise. People who can handle compliance functions might not be able to judge school proposals or interpret data about school success and pupil performance. Individuals who can readily judge the health of a school and understand how to help a struggling operator may not know how to generate interest among competent groups that have never run schools, or connect groups of educators with sources of financial or management expertise. Some individuals (e.g. former D.C. Charter Board leader Nelson Smith, now head of the National Alliance of Public Charter Schools) can handle all these issues, but most authorizers will need to build a diverse team. Team building costs money, of course, but most authorizers already get a share of the per capita funding for schools they oversee.[3]

3. Authorizer economics are Byzantine and sometimes yield perverse incentives. A number of specialized authorizers do *not* get fees from the schools. (A unit of the superintendent's office, the mayor's office, or the state department of education, for example, is not likely to charge sponsorship fees but to cover its chartering costs from

Good authorizer practice is difficult and only a few people have pertinent experience. However, NACSA is emerging as a resource that can provide advice, training, and exemplars for localities seeking to develop capable authorizing agencies. Ohio has developed a "charter sponsor institute" to recruit, train and technically assist new sponsors, especially non-profit organizations, and it has striven with fair success to develop training modules, answers to obvious questions from prospective authorizers (e.g. liability), and a host of common tools and materials that individual sponsors should not have to devise for themselves.

The Future of Authorizing

Charter advocates neglected authorizing at first but are now awakening to its importance. The same cannot be said of conventional school districts and state education departments, which, despite the rhetoric of standards-based reform, have never bothered to figure out how to judge the performance of individual schools or to give themselves (or their students) options if a school is failing. Instead, districts and states continue for the most part to assume that existing public schools are immortal and nothing much can be done about them if they fail, other than to take advantage of staff attrition, tinker with teacher training and add sundry programs on the side.

Charter authorizing points toward a whole new approach to

---

its basic public funding.) Where the sponsor is obliged to subsist on fees, it needs a certain scale of operation, which most sponsorship operations lack, to generate enough fees to build a proper team and infrastructure. This may cause it to be entrepreneurial—or to be less discerning than perhaps it should be about prospective school operators. Moreover, being fee dependent creates a fiscal dilemma for authorizers, when, for example, closing down or not renewing a given school would threaten the sponsor's own fiscal stability. Additionally, in states such as Ohio, where sponsors set their own fees within a legislated range (up to three percent in the Ohio case), schools may shop for low-priced sponsors, but those entities may wind up so fiscally strapped that they cannot afford to do the job well.

public oversight of schooling wherein public authorities take responsibility for judging whether a school is giving children the education they need and for seeking alternatives to consistently low performing schools. A few districts (Chicago, New York, Philadelphia, Milwaukee) and two states (Texas and Florida) have shown some glimmers of interest in performance-based school oversight. But no district is yet overseeing all its schools the way that charter schools are supposed to be overseen.

Today, charters stand apart as the primary example of schools that clearly understand they face oversight that has the power to close or replace them if they do not perform. As noted above, the best examples of responsible charter oversight come from special-purpose authorizers who accept the dual responsibility of using chartering to create new schools while also weeding out low performers. Even those districts that do take that approach to their charters do not apply it to the traditional public schools they operate directly.

Regrettably, however, not all special-purpose authorizers take their work seriously. Like districts, they face conflicting incentives. Even if desirous of promoting good charter schools, they, too, face the temptation to sponsor many schools, then keep them afloat, so as to get oversight fees—and contain the time and cost of reviewing proposals and monitoring school performance. It's not easy or inexpensive to build and maintain the capacity to oversee schools and intervene when things go wrong. As businesses committed to outsourcing have also found, it takes considerable internal capacity to identify good providers and ensure that they perform. A few authorizers (e.g. Central Michigan University) have made the necessary investments in that capacity but many have not.

School districts and special purpose authorizers are also alike in knowing that closing a low performing but popular school can lead to nasty conflicts, adverse publicity and litigation. Only the best authorizers have the fortitude for that tough but necessary part of their roles. State policy matters, too. For example, while the desirability of "multiple authorizers" is a firm tenet of chartering theology—and surely preferable to a single monopolist sponsor whose school decisions cannot be appealed—the emergence of an "authorizer marketplace" may also have perverse consequences. If, for instance, a conscientious sponsor declines to renew an ineffective school, the operator may simply seek a new charter from a different and less persnickety authorizer.

It is possible to remove special purpose authorizers' perverse incentives and encourage them to invest in oversight. If authorizers are themselves accountable to state authorities for the effectiveness of the schools they sponsor, they will be more apt to take quality control seriously. If funded directly by the state, they won't depend on fees from "their" schools.[4] Such policy changes would yield marked improvements in places like Ohio where schools presently pay authorizers variable fees from their operating funds and thus have an incentive to shop for the authorizer that charges the lowest fee (and does the least oversight). If authorizers' decisions—and the performance of their schools—are transparent, media scrutiny and public opinion will provide additional quality control. And if the state has the power to disband or dismiss authorizers that support dismal schools, authorizers will have the incentive to keep out bad schools and take action against low performers.

4. States might, for example, pay special-purpose authorizers fees based on three variables:

- Some basic annual operating support, or core support, for a sponsor that has at least, say, three schools in its portfolio.
- An additional sum for each additional school in its portfolio regardless of size (small amounts, though, to keep the incentive effect within bounds).
- A bonus payment for every school in its portfolio that makes AYP in a given year and/or hits the passing level on a state's own accountability system. (In Ohio, that might mean a school rating of "continuous improvement" or better; in Florida it might be "C" or better.)

It is harder to create the right balance of incentives for school districts. So long as they benefit politically and financially from shielding their traditional schools from competition and strong performance pressures, they will have little incentive to promote charter schools, invest in oversight capacity, or hold all schools to common standards.

The mismatch between the incentives facing districts and special purpose authorizers leaves a big gap in public policy. Districts are ultimately responsible for providing schooling for all the children in their geographic areas, but they can avoid holding schools accountable for performance. Special purpose authorizers are not responsible for any group of children in particular, and even if they do their jobs well there is no guarantee that all the children in the area they serve will be better off. This creates an irrational situation where special purpose authorizers, by doing their job conscientiously, can close schools that are *better* than the options provided to families by the surrounding district. It also allows districts to reject applications from charter operators who would operate better schools than the district's own.

What can be done to create the right mix of incentives for both special purpose authorizers and school districts—and to level this part of the public-education playing field? That important question deserves more than an abstract answer, and we therefore recommend that states experiment with different mixtures of incentives and sanctions for charter authorizers. The broad outlines of a solution are clear, however. It has two parts: (1) generally increasing the quality of authorizer performance and (2) leveling the playing field so that all publicly funded schools, no matter who runs them, are held to the same performance standards. Both of these require state government action and investment, as well as continued participation by private funders, analysts and organizations.

Elements of the first solution include direct state funding of authorizers and state (or privately) supported training and technical assistance for authorizers. Elements of the second solution include the establishment of revocable, results-based accountability contracts (and public transparency) for authorizers themselves.[5] In other words, the state should treat its authorizers more or less the way we hope authorizers will treat schools.[6]

It's also important to lift caps on the numbers of charter schools so that special purpose authorizers can become larger and more capable. This measure alone will not create responsible authorizing. However, in combination with greater accountability for authorizers, it could allow authorizers to develop large enough portfolios of schools, and to receive enough income from state fees, to make serious investments in oversight capacity. If all authorizers (including districts) are held to the same performance standards, a special-purpose sponsor could compete with a district and in time might oversee more schools than the district. Districts, too, would face a need to become good authorizers or risk going of out business altogether.

The federal government has a role here, too. The No Child Left Behind act creates pressure on districts (and states) to provide much tighter oversight of individual school performance—and to deploy charter schools as an option for youngsters otherwise mired in low-performing district-operated schools. Some

5. The first paper to address the issue of oversight and performance incentives for authorizers has just been published. See Robin J. Lake, *Holding Charter School Authorizers Accountable* (Seattle: National Charter School Research Project, 2006).

6. This would include reviews of approval standards for schools and of authorizers' portfolios, leading to de-certification of authorizers that neglect careful screening or school oversight. This is not a new idea, but few states have tried it. Ohio establishes a performance contract between the state department of education and its new special purpose authorizers, akin to the contract between an authorizer and a school. Dean Millot has suggested establishing a state appeal process for charter approval and cancellation decisions. Appeals can be resolved in writing and decisions circulated so they could become precedents affecting future decisions by all authorizers.

districts still think they can beat back the NCLB regimen with complaints about the evils of testing and federal control. Perhaps they'll turn out to be right, but we doubt it, just as we doubt that chartering will go away. But there are two reasons that localities might implement NCLB by *embracing* chartering and using their authority to sponsor charter schools as a model for their oversight of *all* schools. If district leaders place higher priority on providing effective instruction and demonstrable results than on sustaining the current structural arrangements, they will want to oversee schools on the basis of performance and exercise the freedom to abandon an unproductive school in favor of a promising one. Moreover, embracing chartering puts districts in a desirable position *vis a vis* discontented parents and Uncle Sam. Instead of defending schools that don't work—excusing failure by citing funding, regulations, union contracts, etc.—district leaders can regain the initiative. If they adopt performance-based school oversight and develop a steady stream of new school options, they are unlikely to come into conflict with federal regulators—or with disgruntled voters and taxpayers.

To be sure, charter-school authorizing is difficult, and even its most dedicated practitioners are just learning how to do it. But its challenges are finite and tractable. School districts, colleges and universities, city governments and foundations can learn how to do it well, if they will invest in the capacity to oversee schools on the basis of performance. Sound charter authorizing—premised on strong common standards for performance and a level playing field among all publicly funded schools—can be the firm basis for an innovative and continually improving new public education system.

5. Should Charter Schools Be a Cottage Industry?

John E. Chubb

Although no one ever recommended it be so, charter schools have become a cottage industry. Charter schools are small, serving less than 200 students on average—about a third of the size of the typical public school. Charter schools number over 3600 nationwide, with concentrations of nearly a hundred or more schools in ten states.[1] But few of these sizable numbers have joined forces in larger entities to exploit economies of scale. No more than 15 percent of all charter schools are run or supported by management organizations, which work with multiple charter schools. Contrast this with regular public schools, where the average school is part of a system of six schools, and a quarter of all schools are part of systems twice to many times that size.[2] In the fifteen years since the first one was authorized, charter schools have shown a powerful tendency toward small size and total independence.

Is this a good thing? Curiously, the topic has received little

1. Center for Education Reform, Press Release, October 27, 2005.

2. Estimated from the National Center for Education Statistics, *Digest of Education Statistics 2004*, Table 86.

serious attention. Advocates of charter schools have sometimes painted a picture of a proverbial "thousand flowers blooming." And charter schools were certainly intended to give rise to a range of innovative and alternative schools. But charter schools were also founded on the premises of the free market—choice for families and competition among providers generating a new and improved supply of public schools. No economic analysis ever suggested that the market would or should generate mostly small schools, operating independently and enjoying no scale economies. The fact of the matter is debates over charter schools—political and academic alike—never addressed the ideal organization of charter schools. Nobody ever argued that charter schools should become a cottage industry.

Why a Cottage Industry?

The cottage status of the charter industry is, nevertheless, not an accident. Charters are a cottage industry largely because opponents of charter schools want them to be. Since 1991 some forty-one states and the District of Columbia have managed to authorize charter schools. Every piece of charter legislation has been fiercely debated, with opposition coming from the traditional public school world, concerned about the loss of students and revenue, and support coming from uneasy coalitions of business interests, wanting to accelerate school improvement, and community groups, often from inner cities, frustrated with the quality of regular public schools. Every charter law is a compromise. Few laws—less than ten by some estimates and even fewer than that according to the analysis in Caroline Hoxby's chapter in this book—give charter schools opportunity to compete on a level playing field with traditional schools.[3] Opponents are able to limit

3. The Center for Education Reform, the most widely cited evaluator of charter school laws, rates only six laws an "A" and fourteen laws a "B," judging them along

the funding for charters to less than the funding for regular public schools. They are able to cap the number of charters that can operate statewide or in a district. And they are often able to give traditional public schools, the prospective competition for charter schools, control over the granting of charters. These restrictions certainly discourage the growth of charter schools to substantial scale.[4]

But two additional limitations that have become nearly ubiquitous may best explain the scale of charter schooling. One is the ban on for-profit operators of charter schools. At most, three states permit for-profit companies to hold charters directly. Several states also prohibit for-profit companies from contracting with not-for-profit charter holders to provide comprehensive management services. Because for-profit entities generally bring scale to their efforts to maximize profits, the restrictions on for-profit companies reduce the potential for scale to emerge in individual charter schools as well as in systems of charter schools. Opponents of charter schools have long viewed private business as both an inappropriate participant in public education—except as a provider of books, computers, and the like—and as a potential threat to the traditional operators of public schools. That opposition has successfully limited the role of for-profit companies in running charter schools—and thereby kept a lid on the scale of charter operations.

Scale has also been limited by the widespread prohibition upon charter holders of operating more than a single school under one charter. Few states explicitly allow charter holders to operate

---

various dimensions of support for charter school openings. The Center for Education Reform, *The Simple Guide to Charter School Laws: A Progress Report,* Washington, DC: Center for Education Reform, 2005.

4. The political battles associated with new charter legislation and the compromises emerging from those battles have been widely documented. See, for example, Chester E. Finn, Jr., Bruno V. Manno, and Gregg Vanourek, *Charter Schools in Action: Renewing Public Education,* Princeton, NJ: Princeton University Press.

more than a single school. Even those often require each school to have its own board, though boards can occasionally share some members—a "daisy chain" of boards—to facilitate common policies and integrated operations. Most states, however, limit each charter to a single school overseen by a unique board. Such governance requirements ensure that charters cannot become systems—they can only be individual schools. Again, opponents of charters, concerned about the proliferation of well-resourced systems of schools, prefer governance this way—and have successfully lobbied for it in most places. The argument is not that charters will perform best if their scale is limited. The argument is that charters should not threaten the traditional public school system.

Charter schools, then, are a cottage industry not because anyone thought they would do a better job educationally if they were organized this way. Their organization is a byproduct of political opposition and compromise—not conscious design. But does it matter? Would charter schools work better if they could benefit from the direct involvement of business or from economies of scale? More modestly, is there evidence that business involvement and scale operations are a detriment to charter schools, and do they deserve the restrictions now on the books?

Economies of Scale

Although the term "cottage industry" is often used pejoratively, to refer to an enterprise that is exceptionally fragmented and inefficient—though perhaps also quite entrepreneurial—there is nothing inherently wrong with small-scale organization. The appropriate scale of an organization depends on what the organization is trying to do. Five-star restaurants, for example, are almost always small, independent operations. The extraordinary quality found in such establishments depends largely on the individual chef, and gifted chefs do not scale. Grocery stores, by contrast, which also sell food, scale very nicely. Grocery stores with hundreds of sites can offer consumers far lower prices and far more choices than a single "mom and pop" grocery store, and a wider range of quality prepared foods, not unlike a respectable restaurant. National grocery chains have superior purchasing power compared to the independents, and they bring scale economies to all of their operations—from the design of their stores, to the perfection of their operations, to the training and development of their staff.

Whether an enterprise should be small scale, as with five-star restaurants, or large scale, as with grocery stores, depends on many factors. Can the core competence of the enterprise be replicated through strong systems and processes? Do the marginal costs of producing more of the goods or services generally decrease with larger and larger volumes? Is the mission of the organization to serve large numbers? *Private* enterprises regularly ask these questions—and then try out their answers in the marketplace. If scale is beneficial, consumers flock to the larger enterprises for their lower prices, their higher quality, and their greater convenience—or whatever mix of benefits that consumers value. If scale does not offer benefits that consumer value, smaller scale enterprises prevail. Over the last century, consumers have clearly chosen large scale over small for a wide range of goods and services: food, clothing, finance, transportation, communication, and more. Yet, it is also true that small businesses are a major part of today's economy, serving, for example, as a greater source of new jobs than big businesses. The free market values enterprises large and small.

The Politics of Scale

What about schools? First, and foremost, we do not have the benefit of the market to evaluate the ideal scale of schooling. Public schools are products not of market forces but of public policy. Public education is provided as a public good in the United States as in most countries. It is in the public interest—few would disagree—to ensure that every child receive an education sufficient to prepare him or her to be a responsible citizen and a productive adult. Education is therefore provided freely and universally in most countries. As a public good, education can be provided in various ways, and countries do differ in this respect. Most importantly, education can be provided exclusively through schools run by the government. Or education can be provided by funding private, parochial, and other types of schools—for example, charter schools—with tax dollars, as well as setting up government-run schools. Until very recently, all public education in the United States was provided through government-run schools.

The scale of public schooling in the United States has therefore been largely a matter of public policy. To be specific, state policy establishes the fiscal and educational requirements for local school districts, and district policy determines the size of schools. A century ago, public schooling was generally small scale. With the exception of major city school systems, public schooling was community-based, every community having democratic control over its own schools. Some 100,000 school systems dotted the national landscape, many containing but a single school. "One-room school houses" serving students at multiple grades with a single teacher were very common. The average public school system had barely two schools with each serving a little over 200 students.

Over the last century, however, the scale of public schooling changed decisively. In the early 1900s, education authorities from leading universities, the business community, and the governing elite, began to argue for a more "scientific" organization of schools.[5] They wanted schools less influenced by the political prerogatives of amateur school boards, less dependent on the wiles of the individual classroom teacher, and more driven by planning, systems, and specialization. Students needed differentiated programs, teachers needed prescribed curricula and formal training, and schools needed the support of sophisticated professionals including a superintendent and an expert staff.[6]

To be organized scientifically, schools and school systems needed greater scale. Over the course of the twentieth century, school systems were consolidated to create less than 15,000 systems from the original 100,000. Schools grew in size, more than doubling to over 500 students on average. High schools were especially affected as more and more adopted the post-war "comprehensive" model providing students with programs tailored to their post-high school aspirations, from business to vocational to college.

The impact of all of this consolidation on school performance is an unsettled issue. The comprehensive high school has certainly come in for strong criticism in recent years for being too large and impersonal. The biggest school systems in America, serving mostly major cities, have long been criticized as too politicized, too bureaucratized, and largely unsuccessful. The effects of district consolidation on rural education have not been clearly positive. One might say that while the question is unresolved, it is not clear that scale is an answer for what ails America's schools.[7]

5. The development of the modern school system is well explained in David B. Tyack, *The One Best System: A History of American Urban Education,* Cambridge, MA: Harvard University Press, 1974.

6. Augmenting these arguments were concerns about schools falling under the control of waves of immigrants flooding the cities.

7. On the impact of school and district consolidation see Paul E. Peterson, "Con-

Yet, that would be jumping to a conclusion because scale has been put to a very different kind of test in public education than in private enterprises. Scale has not been put to a market test; it has passed a political test. Schools and school systems are the scale that state and local politics, through time and compromise, have caused them to be. Schooling is not organized to maximize what consumers—be they students, families, or taxpayers—value. The closest we have to a market test of educational scale is private schools, which tend to be small and independent. But the private market is widely dispersed and serves only ten percent of all students and only families with the ability to pay. There is no telling what scale public schooling might assume if we allowed a family-driven market to determine its organization.

This is the crucial point: with charter schools, the nation has a potential vehicle for exploring the ideal scale for public schooling. The organization of public schooling heretofore has been determined entirely by politics. This is appropriate to a degree since public schools must be ultimately accountable to democratic authority. But politics need not be the only determinant of how education is organized and delivered. It is a high price to pay for education to remain the only important enterprise in American society for which we have so little idea how scale or alternative forms of organization might benefit its delivery. Charter schools could provide a test of how scale might or might not benefit education, but the test has been hampered by the limitations on scale imposed by charter laws—by politics.

The Potential of Scale

Consider the budget of a typical charter school with, say, 200 students. Assume (see Table 5.1) the school is funded with

---

solidate Districts not Schools," in Koret Task Force, *Reforming Education in Arkansas*, Stanford, CA: Hoover Institution Press, 2005.

Table 5.1 Annual Budget of Typical Charter School

Revenue	
200 Students @ $9,000 per student	$1,800,000
Personnel Expenses (including benefits)	
Teachers: 15 @ $60,000 per	$900,000
Principal	$100,000
Counselor	$75,000
Nurse (part time)	$25,000
Technology Manager	$75,000
Administrative Assistants: 2 @ $50,000 per	$100,000
Total Personnel	$1,275,000
Non-personnel Expenses	
Rent or Mortgage	$250,000
Furniture (amortized over five years)	$20,000
Durable books, materials, equipment (amortized over five years)	$30,000
Computers and lab technology (amortized over five years)	$10,000
Non-durable instructional supplies	$20,000
Office supplies, copier rental	$20,000
Contracted professional services (e.g., psychologist)	$25,000
Legal fees	$25,000
Utilities	$50,000
Maintenance	$75,000
Total Non-personnel Expenses	$525,000
Total Expenses	$1,800,000
Surplus	$100,000

roughly the national average per pupil revenue of $9,000, which provides the school total funding of $1.8 million. If the typical class size in the school is twenty, the school will need ten core teachers, plus another three teachers of non-core subjects (e.g., art, music, physical education, etc.) to provide the core teachers—and themselves—one to two planning periods per day. If we assume that 12 percent of the students—the national average—require special education services, the school will need two special education teachers, each with a case load of twelve students. The total teaching staff therefore will number fifteen. If each is paid the national average salary of about $47,000 with typical benefits of 25 percent of base, each teacher costs approximately $60,000. Total cost of teaching staff: $900,000.

The school will require additional personnel. A principal will cost $100,000 including benefits. The school will almost certainly want a counselor—another $75,000. A part-time nurse is usually necessary—at least $25,000. If the school employs technology, it will want the hardware and software maintained—another $75,000. The front office needs student information recorded, reports produced, phones answered, and parents greeted: two administrative assistants, $100,000. Total "non-instructional" staff: $375,000. Total personnel costs for the small charter school: $1.275 million.

On the non-personnel side the biggest cost is rent or mortgage. Students on average require at least 100 square feet per pupil—and that would be tight by most new public school standards. Minimum school size then would be 20,000 square feet. A new facility would cost at least $2 million to construct, plus land, which could be assumed to value a quarter of construction costs, or $500,000. A $2.5 million new facility could be financed, but at rather high interest rates, say 10 percent, because charter schools are only authorized for five years at a time. Even an interest-only loan imposes a $250,000 burden on the budget. Market rents would be in the same ballpark based on replacement costs.

Students need books, equipment, and computers, which averages $750 per student for grades K–8. The total cost of $150,000 can be spread over five years for an annual cost of $30,000. A computer lab with server runs another $50,000, which also can be spread over five years, for a yearly hit of $10,000. Schools must be furnished with desks, chairs, bookcases, etc. Average cost for a school this size is $100,000, which amortized comes to $20,000 annually. Nondurable materials, like workbooks, paper, and art supplies cost about $100 per student, or $20,000 per year. Instructional materials, furniture, and equipment totals $80,000. Office supplies, photocopier rentals, and the like add another $20,000 per year to a typical small school. Total supply bill: $100,000.

The services of psychologists, speech pathologists, and other specialists required for special education services not provided by school staff demand $25,000 be set aside for contracted services. Charter schools inevitably face legal fees, especially associated with special education; $25,000 is a conservative estimate. Schools have utility bills, which for a 20,000 square feet school could easily cost $50,000 per year. Maintenance, assuming one full-time custodian and night-time cleaning under contract to a school maintenance firm, costs at least $75,000. The total cost of contract services, legal, utilities, and maintenance: $175,000.

The total annual expenses of this very typical charter are $1.8 million. This sum assumes that the school does not provide transportation or food. It also assumes it is not a high school, which would be even more expensive. What remains, if the school does a superb job of watching its expenses, is a surplus of $100,000. With this the school must do everything else necessary to meet state and federal academic standards, fulfill all other commitments of its charter, and compete successfully with traditional public schools. But what can a school do on its own for $100,000 to improve its performance? The answer is not very much.

Schools—meaning teachers and principals—need help with a wide range of issues that govern their success. How should a curriculum be constructed to maximize student success on the standards of a particular state? What should be done about the achievement of disadvantaged students who are not responding to published reading programs? How shall students be assessed on an ongoing basis? How should standardized test data be interpreted? How shall student management be handled? As students get older and the subjects more demanding, where do teachers turn for advice in the sciences, the branches of mathematics, and different fields of literature? If managing data and instructional information requires technology, who is going to handle the necessary technology systems and their integration? If we want to assume that the teachers and other professionals in the schools will bring some of these skills with them, how do we assume the schools will recruit and hire the very best education staff when great educators are very hard to find?

The answer to all of these questions is that the school's $100,000 will not go very far. The school can hire a curriculum, instruction, and assessment specialist for the whole sum—hoping to find a brilliant jack of all trades; it could send the entire staff to two professional meetings a year, or it could buy professional development and consulting, which might meet a need or two annually. Basically, the $100,000 surplus will not allow the school to do the research, to develop the solutions and systems, and to address the many challenges it will inevitably have. The school will be left to depend, much like schools a century ago, almost entirely on the wiles of its own staff.

But schools do not have to suffer for lack of crucial support services. If schools are banded together, or if schools themselves are larger in size, economies of scale are possible. Larger schools are not proportionately expensive. Almost every cost except teachers declines on a per student basis. The "surplus" of a 500 student school could very easily be $500,000. More dramatically, the sum of the surpluses of multiple schools could fund a serious support organization, with the specialists necessary to meet key school instructional needs. A support organization paid a fee of $500,000 per 500 student school would be a $25 million operation if it served only fifty schools. That kind of scale is still small by the standards of corporate America, but it is great by the standards of public education. The average public school is part of a system of only six schools. Three-fourths of all public schools are served by systems with less than fifteen schools.[8] Even the larger school systems do not devote anything like $25 million to support services focused on curriculum, instruction, and assessment.

Comprehensive support organizations should be able to offer charter schools a range of educational services at a much lower total price and a much higher quality level than schools would find if they tried to provide the services themselves or tried to purchase them individually from multiple vendors. Schools do not have the resources to develop serious expertise in any of the specialized areas of knowledge crucial to school success, nor do they have systems to ensure consistent and effective execution. Scale organizations do. And when scale organizations offer comprehensive services, they enjoy additional economies. Field staff can be trained to provide multiple forms of support to their schools. Training conferences can address a wide range of needs. Schools are therefore likely to find it more efficient to purchase support—assuming they need multiple forms of support—from comprehensive organizations than from specialized ones. Educational support organizations have traditionally been set up on a specialized basis, offering discrete services such as curriculum alignment, data analysis, student assessment, special education, classroom management, leadership development, and a long list of other training needs. With the advent of charter schools, however, the comprehensive model of service provision has become increasingly popular.

Charter schools and charter advocates are beginning to recognize the potential of comprehensive service providers—and scale. In California, one of the leading charter states with over 500 charter schools, serious organizations have sprouted to support multiple charter schools. The New Schools Venture Fund,

8. Estimated from National Center for Education Statistics, *Digest of Education Statistics 2004*, Table 86.

an investment philanthropy capitalized with some $15 million, is funding the start up of what are becoming known as Charter Management Organizations (or CMOs). These not-for-profit entities, which include Aspire Schools, Green Dot Schools, and the Knowledge is Power Program (or KIPP), among others, aim to provide bundles of well-researched and highly developed educational services that charter schools could never provide themselves and could never buy effectively unbundled or ala carte. KIPP, for example, offers an exceptional leadership development program. Other philanthropies such as Pisces (funded by the Fisher family, founders of The Gap) and the Walton Foundation are funding the leading CMOs and cultivating new ones. These prominent philanthropies, like growing numbers of charter advocates, believe that charter schools will perform better if each school does not have to solve every problem on its own—if each school can benefit from scale educational services organizations.

The Benefits of For-Profit Scale Organizations

The CMO movement represents one form of scale organization—the not-for-profit form. But scale can obviously come from organizations with the same mission as CMOs but organized on a for-profit basis. For-profits have come to be known by the similar title of Educational Management Organizations (or EMOs). What might they add to the potential benefits of scale organizations?

For-profit organizations have a natural tendency to push scale economies to their limit. As long as the mission of a for-profit organization is to provide its services as widely as possible—a grocery chain, for example, and not a five star restaurant—a for-profit organization wants to reach scale. With scale come operating efficiencies, additional revenue, and greater profits—in absolute terms and as a percentage of profits. For-profit organizations seek to maximize profit and, thereby, scale. But they don't do so without limits. In a proper market they must compete with other organizations for customers—a process that rewards quality service and drives profit down. As consumers of for-profit services, charter schools would be the ultimate beneficiaries of a market for service providers. Schools would receive the best service that scale can offer and at the lowest price. If a for-profit operator tried to skimp on quality to increase profits, it would lose business to operators who did not reduce quality at the same price. This all assumes, of course, a free market for for-profit charter support organizations—which does not fully exist.

For-profits have another potential advantage over not-for-profits. For-profits tend to have much greater access to the capital needed to get to scale. Launching and building an organization requires investment or philanthropy. No business of any scale pays for its own operations from opening day. The advantage of for-profits is that they can raise capital in the private market where vastly more funds are available than through philanthropy. Investors put money in for-profit organizations to help them get started, to grow, or to develop the next great innovation because they hope to get a return on their investments. Donors put money in philanthropies because they want to help a cause that the market does not usually support, and they, unlike investors, do not expect anything in return. Organizations that can promise investors a return on their money usually have a far easier time attracting funds than organizations looking for gifts.

For-profits, then, should have more motive and better means than not-for-profits to get to scale. But not-for-profits have their own advantages, particularly in the support of charter schools, in beating for-profits on price. The not-for-profit needs about 8% less revenue because it is not seeking to make money, and it can also subsidize its services with philanthropy. For example, with generous philanthropic support, schools supported by KIPP have budgets that sometimes exceed per pupil public revenue. The schools pay KIPP, but KIPP tops off the paid services with offerings paid with philanthropy. Not-for-profits also have advantages under current charter law: they can hold charters directly while for-profits generally cannot.

The Evidence: Scaling Up

Although scale organizations, both for-profit and not-for-profit, have been limited by existing charter law, they have not been thwarted altogether. Over the nearly fifteen year history of charter schools, scale organizations have accumulated enough of a track record to suggest what their contributions may ultimately be. Many organizations have been in existence since the mid-1990s and are now working with charter schools in over half of the states that authorize charters. In 2004–2005 roughly 600 schools were supported by organizations that work with at least four schools overall.

Which raises a question of terminology: what is a scale support organization? Why would one consider an organization that works with only four schools a scale operation? Putting first things first, the focus here is not on just any kind of scale educational enterprise. Charter schools can and do buy their books and computers from major businesses that operate at enormous scale. They may also buy discrete services from other specialized scale vendors like bus companies, food service providers, payroll companies, testing firms, and the like. The focus here is on CMOs and EMOs, organizations with the expertise to help charter schools with every aspect of their educational mission—classroom management, curriculum, instruction, assessment, technology, data analysis, special education, family and community. These organizations often fully manage or run the school for the charter holder. They frequently apply their services in accordance with an integrated model of how the entire school should work. But they are also relatively new enterprises, still seeking scale—which is why four schools are sufficient to warrant consideration in this analysis. Organizations with fewer than four schools are simply too small to track reliably.

One final clarification: some of the organizations with four or more schools also work with non-charter public schools, through comprehensive management agreements with school districts. The data on the scale and scope of the organizations considered here does not attempt to separate out non-charter contracts because the information to do so is not always available. In any case, if work with non-charters is part of the process of getting to scale, organizations that follow such a route should not be downplayed—they are still establishing scale. However, to avoid any confusion about what is most important, the subsequent analysis of organizational effectiveness will look only at charters. All data are through the 2004–2005 school year.

Table 5.2 displays the distribution of management organizations by the geographic scope of their operations. Several patterns stand out. First, there is a strong tendency toward geographic concentration. Over half of the management organizations—eighteen out of thirty-two—work in only a single state. Only seven organizations work in more than five states. There are several possible explanations for this pattern. One is that some of the not-for-profits, especially the universities, have no mission to work beyond their local community. They might some day work in a significant number of local schools and develop true scale operations, but they would never work beyond their immediate borders. Another explanation is time. Most of these organizations have less than ten years' experience offering comprehensive services; they may not have had time to scale beyond a state or two, though they will eventually. The truth of this is unknowable.

The final reason for geographic specialization may be the nature of public education itself. Controlled by the states, public

Table 5.2 Geographic Distribution of School Management Organizations with Four or More Schools (School locations operating in the 2004–2005 School Year)

	Location	*Number of States*
For-Profit Management Organizations[a]		
Edison Schools, Inc.	CA, CO, DC, DE, GA, IA, IL, IN, MA, MD, MI, MN, MO, NV, NY, OH, PA, WI	18
Imagine Schools	AZ, DC, FL, GA, MA, MI, MO, NC, NY	9
K12, Inc.	AZ, CA, CO, DC, FL, ID, OH, PA, WI	9
Mosaica Schools	AZ, CO, DC, DE, IN, MI, NY, OH, PA	9
Connections Academy	AZ, CA, CO, FL, OH, PA, WI	7
SABIS Educational Systems	AZ, LA, MA, MI, MN, NY, OH	7
National Heritage Academies	IN, MI, NC, NY, OH	5
Richard Milburn High School, Inc.	TX, FL, IL, NC, VA	5
White Hat Management	AZ, CO, MI, OH	4
Charter School Administrative Services	FL, MI, MO, TX	4
The Leona Group, LLC	AZ, IN, MI, OH	4
Victory Schools, Inc.	MD, NY, PA	3
Charter Schools USA	FL, TX	2
Designs for Learning, Inc.	MN	1
Helicon Associaties	MI	1
The Planagement Group	TX	1
Sequoia Charter Schools	AZ	1
Choice Schools, Associates	MI	1
Excel Education Centers, Inc.	AZ	1
Ideabanc, Inc.	AZ	1
Nobel Learning Communities	PA	1
Ombudsman Educational Service, Ltd.	AZ	1
Pinnacle Education, Inc.	AZ	1
The Romine Group, Inc.	MI	1
For Profit Averages		4.08
Not-For-Profit Management Organizations[b]		
KIPP – Knowledge is Power Program	AR, CA, CO, DC, GA, IL, IN, MA, MD, NC, NJ, NY, OK, PA, TN, TX	16
Boston University	MA	1
Foundations, Inc.	PA	1
Temple University	PA	1
Universal Charter Schools	PA	1
University of Pennsylvania	PA	1
Aspire Public Schools	CA	1
Green Dot Public Schools	CA	1
Not For Profit Averages		2.67

[a] Source: Molnar, Alex et. al. (2005), *Profiles of For-Profit Education Management Organizations: Seventh-Annual Report*, Commercialism in Education Research Unit- Education Policy Studies Laboratory, Arizona State University, http://edpolicylab.org

[b] Based on Schools Reported in Education Management Organization Websites

education differs a great deal from state to state as gauged by academic standards, high-stakes assessments, school law, program regulations, and school culture. Support organizations need to master the details of each state's education system—and this takes major resources. An organization would seem more likely to scale and succeed if it focused on a small number of states it could perform in exceedingly well. For the most part, management organizations have concentrated geographically, which is probably a good thing for improving schools since expertise matters.

Yet, some organizations have chosen to set up shop in many states. Seven CMOs or EMOs are working in seven or more states. Two organizations, Edison and KIPP, are in eighteen and sixteen states respectively. What can we say about the tendency to try and serve multiple states? It is clearly a tendency of for-profit firms. Six of the seven organizations working in seven or more states are trying to make a profit. Only one of the fourteen organizations operating in more than one state—KIPP—is a not-for-profit.[9] What the data unmistakably show is that while there is a preference among all organizations for geographic specialization, the for-profit firms have frequently chosen or been driven to expand their operations beyond single states. To be sure, KIPP is evidence that a not-for-profit can approach national scope; it is second to Edison in state penetration. But KIPP notwithstanding, for-profits and not-for-profits seem to prefer different geographic playing fields. As the table shows, the average for-profit is working in half again as many states (4.08 vs. 2.67) as the average not-for-profit. Whether geographic spread is a good thing or a bad thing educationally is another matter, considered subsequently. But first, let's consider some additional aspects of getting to scale.

9. At this writing Imagine Schools was reportedly in the process of converting from for-profit to not-for-profit status. But because it built its school portfolio as a for-profit organization, it is considered for-profit here.

Table 5.3 depicts EMOs and CMOs by initial year of operation, total enrollment, number of schools, and average school size. A few patterns are very plain. First, EMOs and CMOs have been around for the same amount of time on average with both sectors' modal operations commencing in the mid-1990s. Despite the same amounts of time on the scene, for-profit firms have achieved more scale than not-for-profit organizations. The average EMO works with 20.1 schools; the average CMO works with half that number, or 10.1 schools. The average EMO serves 9,232 students; the average CMO serves less than a quarter of that or 2,051 students. Compared to public school systems, EMOs are reaching the scale of mid-size school systems while CMOs are currently more like small school systems. The EMOs also include several firms that have reached the scale of moderate to major school systems. It is too early to tell what scale for-profit and not-for-profit support organizations will ultimately reach. None has been operating long enough to have established a growth plateau. But it seems safe to say that for-profits are moving toward scale more rapidly than not-for-profits.

Another trend that bears watching still is school size. The averages do not show great differences between for-profits and not-for-profits. The average school served by for-profits enrolls 373 students; the average school served by not-for-profits enrolls 300. This difference is in the expected direction. Larger schools are more efficient and generate more of a surplus than smaller schools. For-profit firms have more need, since they lack philanthropy, to work with schools that can pay their own way. And several of the larger EMOs tend to work in significantly bigger schools than the EMO average—serving 500–700 students.[10] But these numbers are not all that large when compared to the national average of all public schools, which approaches 600.

10. The average enrollment in K12 schools exceeds 900 because these schools are virtual, attended via the Internet.

Table 5.3 Longevity and Size of School Management Organizations with Four or More Schools (School Year 2004–2005)

	First School	*Number of Schools*	*Total Enrolled*	*Average School Size*
For-Profit Management Organizations[a]				
Edison Schools, Inc.	1996	98	66482	678
National Heritage Academies	1995	51	26133	512
The Leona Group, LLC	1995	45	13990	311
White Hat Management	1998	38	18318	482
Imagine Schools	1996	33	18194	551
Mosaica Schools	1997	27	9995	370
Charter Schools USA	1999	18	11205	623
Richard Milburn High School, Inc.	1989	18	4339	241
The Planagement Group	1998	18	2301	128
Charter School Administrative Services	1995	15	7295	486
K12, Inc.	2001	15	14460	964
Helicon Associaties	1995	14	5522	394
Victory Schools, Inc.	1999	13	5683	437
Sequoia Charter Schools	1996	11	1552	141
Connections Academy	2002	10	1081	108
Designs for Learning, Inc.	1996	10	1485	149
Pinnacle Education, Inc.	1995	9	1327	147
Choice Schools, Associates	1994	8	1825	228
Excel Education Centers, Inc.	1995	8	687	86
SABIS Educational Systems	1995	7	4660	666
Ombudsman Educational Service, Ltd.	1996	5	448	90
Ideabanc, Inc.	1998	4	1384	346
Nobel Learning Communities	1999	4	2109	527
The Romine Group, Inc.	2002	4	1095	274
For-Profit Averages	1997	20.1	9232	373
Not-For-Profit Management Organizations[b]				
Knowledge Is Power Program (KIPP)	1995	38	3461	91
Aspire Public Schools	1999	11	944	86
Boston University	1989	10	3826	383
Foundations, Inc.	1992	5	2173	435
Green Dot Public Schools	2000	5	1482	296
Temple University	1991	5	2029	406
Universal Charter Schools	1999	4	1482	371
University of Penn	2001	3	1009	336
Not-For-Profit Averages	1996	10.1	2051	300

[a] Source: Molnar, Alex et. al. (2005), *Profiles of For-Profit Education Management Organizations: Seventh-Annual Report*, Commercialism in Education Research Unit- Education Policy Studies Laboratory, Arizona State University, http://edpolicylab.org

[b] Based on Schools Reported in Education Management Organization Websites

The more striking deviations from sector averages are two prominent CMOs, KIPP and Aspire. Their schools are absolutely tiny, averaging only ninety-one and eighty-six students respectively. KIPP and Aspire want them this way. They build their schools slowly but surely, grade by grade, over a period of years, and reach capacities well below national averages. This approach requires substantial external support, as tiny schools are not efficient. But with philanthropy, it has certainly proven workable: KIPP in particular is second only to Edison in number of states served and fifth in number of schools operated. KIPP served less than 4,000 students in 2004–2005, but its footprint was all over the nation. Time will tell whether the gradual roll-out of small schools is a viable strategy, with philanthropic support, for helping large numbers of charter schools succeed.

To recap, for-profit support organizations tend to pursue scale faster and more widely than not-for-profit organizations. For-profits do this by scaling up their own operations rather than dramatically scaling up their individual schools. But who do the different sectors serve as they pursue new customers? Are they reaching out to kids in clear need? The purpose of charter legislation, after all, is to offer alternatives to students who often do not have them, particularly the economically disadvantaged. Table 5.4 helps answer that question.

Both sectors tend to serve students who are more diverse and more disadvantaged than public schools generally. Most obviously, African Americans make up 35 percent of the for-profit enrollment and 53 percent of the not-for-profit enrollment versus a national average enrollment for African Americans of 13 percent. Poverty has a similar tendency. Students eligible for free or reduced-price lunch represent 54 percent of the for-profit enrollment and 71 percent of the not-for-profit enrollment; the national public school average is only 38 percent. The not-for-profit sector is enrolling a more diverse and needier group of students

Table 5.4 Demographics of School Management Organizations with Four or More Schools (Demographic Data from the 2003–2004 school year)[a]

	Percent African American	*Percent Hispanic*	*Percent White*	*Percent Free/Reduced-Price Lunch*
For-Profit Management Organizations[a]				
Charter Schools USA	29.8	24.4	44.1	100.0
Connections Academy	5.9	2.9	90.3	100.0
Charter School Administrative Services	93.6	5.0	0.7	98.0
Victory Schools, Inc.	92.5	4.2	1.2	89.4
Edison Schools, Inc.	67.3	20.4	10.4	69.2
Mosaica Schools	56.7	34.6	27.2	63.8
Choice Schools, Associates	41.9	4.1	52.3	56.4
Designs for Learning, Inc.	38.8	8.0	42.4	55.5
White Hat Management	68.4	2.6	26.5	47.4
Richard Milburn High School, Inc.	29.6	26.8	42.6	42.7
Helicon Associaties	39.3	7.3	46.4	41.7
Imagine Schools	37.5	17.5	41.5	40.8
The Leona Group, LLC	38.6	32.0	24.9	37.8
National Heritage Academies	29.9	6.2	61.4	29.7
The Romine Group, Inc.	18.4	4.7	72.9	19.2
Nobel Learning Communities	29.4	5.1	64.5	16.6
SABIS Educational Systems	49.8	16.7	32.1	10.8
The Planagement Group	n/a	n/a	n/a	n/a
Ideabanc, Inc.	14.4	41.4	38.2	n/a
Pinnacle Education, Inc.	8.9	42.3	42.5	n/a
Sequoia Charter Schools	6.5	18.8	70.6	n/a
K12, Inc.	4.9	4.0	85.0	n/a
Ombudsman Educational Service, Ltd.	3.7	19.5	71.5	n/a
Excel Education Centers, Inc.	0.8	13.9	63.4	n/a
For-Profit Demographic Average	35.1	15.8	45.8	54.1
Not-For-Profit Management Organizations[b]				
Boston University	6.8	71.8	15.6	n/a
KIPP	37.2	34.4	2.8	68.6
Foundations, Inc.	98.6	0.8	0.5	86.4
Temple University	82.9	11.1	0.7	96.2
Universal Charter Schools	89.3	1.0	3.4	76.9
University of Pennsylvania	93.0	1.3	1.4	90.8
Aspire Public Schools	3.1	44.5	41.6	11.2
Green Dot Public Schools	13.7	85.7	0.6	65.3
Not-For-Profit Demographic Average	53.1	31.3	8.3	70.8

[a] Based on the Nation Center for Education Statistics Demographic Data for the 2003–2004 School Year

[b] Based on school listings from organization websites, cross referenced with the Nation Center for Education Statistics Demographic Data for the 2003–2004 School Year

than the for-profits, on average, but the differences between the sectors are considerably smaller than the differences between schools run by management organizations and public schools generally.

It is also the case that some of the largest providers in each sector tend disproportionately to serve students who have traditionally not been served well by public schools. Among CMOs, KIPP students are 82 percent eligible for free or reduced-price lunch; Green Dot students are 85 percent eligible; Universal students are 81 percent eligible. Among EMOs, Charter Schools USA students are 100 percent eligible; Victory students are 89 percent eligible; Edison students are 69 percent eligible. Critics of business participation in charter schooling have argued that firms might exploit the poor: the poor are the most desperate for alternatives to their traditional public schools and least able to evaluate the quality of what a new provider might offer. But the data do not show such a pattern. For-profits, like not-for-profits, serve needier students than the national average by far. This indicates that both groups are reaching the students that charter schools are supposed to reach. But there is no evidence that for-profits are somehow trying to capture a niche of the poorest of the poor. Not-for-profits on average serve the students who are very most in need.

The Evidence: Student Achievement

Any policy that stands to affect the operation of charter schools ought to be evaluated by how it affects students—particularly their achievement. Unfortunately, policies concerning scale organizations historically have been based on the arguments of political opponents and not on hard evidence of effects of any kind. Opponents have argued successfully that scale organizations will weaken public control over charter schools and that for-profit organizations will put profits ahead of students. Opponents have persuaded policymakers that large entities, whether for profit or not, will behave in ways that are likely to compromise educational quality. Yet, it is also clear that through economies of scale an organization supporting many schools might be able to provide those schools far more and better services than any school could provide or purchase on its own. The key questions, then, are really empirical. How do scale organizations actually behave and what difference do they make for students?

To begin, the data indicate that management organizations have not generally committed the sins that opponents feared they would commit—going national, driving up school size, serving the easy-to-serve. The data also indicate that for-profits are scaling more rapidly than not-for-profits. If it turns out that scale organizations are helping charter schools, then understanding how organizations get to scale may prove helpful. But the decisive data for making good policy regarding charter schools is data on student achievement.

Table 5.5 displays the data necessary to evaluate the academic progress of schools working with management organizations. Under the federal government's *No Child Left Behind (NCLB)* legislation, passed in 2002, all states are required to administer reading and math assessments to all students in grades 3–8 inclusive and one grade of high school, every year beginning in 2005–2006. Prior to that time states were permitted to test fewer grade levels each year, but all states had begun annual testing during the 1990s. States had also written their tests to measure achievement of explicit academic standards and to gauge student progress toward a demanding definition of "proficiency"—all later required by *NCLB*. State tests therefore provide increasingly common metrics for analyzing student achievement across the nation. State standards and tests differ in difficulty, to be sure, but they bring a singular perspective to assessment—annual measurement of

Table 5.5 Academic Gains in Management Organizations with Four or More Schools (Percent Proficient or Advanced – Reading and Math on State Assessments 2002–2005[a]

		Schools in Sample			Manager Gains			State Gains			Relative Manager Gains		
	No. of Schools	*1 year*	*2 years*	*3 years*	*1 year*	*2 years*	*3 years*	*1 year*	*2 years*	*3 years*	*1 year*	*2 years*	*3 years*
For-Profit Management Organizations[b]													
Edison Schools Inc.[a]	51	44	39	25	5.62	10.41	14.60	3.56	7.53	8.20	2.06	2.88	6.40
National Heritage Academies[a]	51	38	33	28	4.53	9.41	19.36	−1.53	5.02	5.92	6.06	4.39	13.44
Leona Group LLC[a]	45	38	30	26	12.06	14.53	19.67	3.70	2.09	6.26	8.36	12.44	13.41
White Hat Management	36	26	19	12	10.83	20.09	21.79	4.79	8.68	8.11	6.04	11.41	13.68
Imagine Schools	31	29	26	20	8.90	11.00	11.60	1.24	3.92	6.65	7.66	7.08	4.95
Mosaica Schools[a]	27	19	14	9	3.25	9.91	16.91	−0.14	4.94	6.63	3.39	4.97	10.28
Charter Schools USA	18	11	9	6	6.45	4.48	13.87	1.73	3.92	8.83	4.72	0.56	5.04
Richard Milburn Academies	15	14	11	3	−2.02	2.67	−1.42	−0.54	1.82	4.50	−1.48	0.85	−5.92
For-Profit Average Gains	274	219	181	129	6.20	10.31	14.55	1.60	4.74	6.89	4.60	5.57	7.66
Non-Profit Management Organizations[b]													
KIPP[a]	52	24	9	1	8.75	10.39	3.00	2.02	1.89	4.75	6.73	8.50	−1.75
Aspire Public Schools	11	10	8	4	9.64	10.33	19.30	4.25	4.62	10.01	5.39	5.71	9.29
Not-For-Profit Average Gains	63	34	17	5	9.20	10.36	11.15	3.14	3.26	7.38	6.06	7.11	3.77

[a] In Indiana, Fall 2005–2006 ISTEP+ results are used to provide one-year gains for this analysis. Edison Schools, National Heritage, Leona, and Mosaica each have one charter school in Indiana.

[b] Based on schools listed in official websites and cross-referencing with 2004–2005 state test result reports.

achievement in reading and math at consecutive grade levels calibrated against an objective standard of proficiency.

Table 5.5 presents average reading and math scores on state tests measured as gains against proficiency. The focus is on gains rather than on absolute scores because we want to know whether the charter school or its manager is adding any value. If a school in its first year of operation posts a score of, say, 50 percent proficient, there is no easy way to evaluate the score. If the students were very bright upon arrival, a 50 percent success rate would be terrible. If the students had historically been very weak, a 50 percent success rate would be very good. To know whether the school is making a difference for students, the simplest test is to see if the school helps more kids achieve proficiency each year. Comparing scores from year to year—calculating gains—gives a rough measure of the effect that the school is having on student achievement.

Gains alone do not tell the whole story, however. For many reasons—from student experience with tests to adjustments in state proficiency standards to the state release of information to help schools prepare for tests—scores can move upward without students really learning anything more. If a school, for example, posted a 5 percentage point gain in its proficiency score, but every school in the state did the same thing, the gain would hardly be an indicator that the school was doing anything special. Accordingly, it is useful to look not only at gains, but gains relative to average gains by the whole state. Table 5.5 does this as well.[11] Finally, test scores have a certain element of random error in

11. The state gains are weighted to reflect the grade levels served by the managers in a given state. For example, if managers in a state served mostly elementary schools, the elementary grades would dominate the state gain averages. An even more rigorous analysis of gains would look at gains by schools in comparison to gains by demographically and academically similar schools. With hundreds of management-supported schools in this analysis, the number of comparable schools that would need to be identified would number in the thousands—beyond the scope of this research.

them. Students would not post identical scores if they took the same test multiple times. As a result, the average scores of schools tend to move up and down randomly depending upon underlying trends in student learning. To not be misled by random fluctuations that could lead gains to be unusually high or low in a single year, Table 5.5 also presents data for two- and three-year gains. The three-year gains are for 2002–2005; the two-year gains for 2003–2005; and the one-year gains for 2004–2005.[12]

What do the data reveal? First, the charter schools operated by all managers are making academic gains against their state proficiency standards. Over a three-year span many of the gains are in double digits, which is close to what *NCLB* demands in lower performing schools. No manager has test scores showing no progress. Given all of the failure in public education, it is striking that not a single manager is failing on average to make academic progress.

But how impressive is the progress? All of the states in which the managers work have also been making gains. Typical gains are two percentage points per year, though higher in some states. When the average state gains are subtracted from the respective manager gains, the manager gains are less impressive than in their absolute form. In relative terms, the results are generally positive. With only a few exceptions managers are posting one-, two-, and three-year gains greater than state averages. Since the positive findings are not only evident in one year data, it is clear that the relative gains are not short-term flukes. The long term data are pretty clear evidence that management organizations can help charter schools perform better than state norms.

Does it matter whether the management organization is for-profit or not-for-profit? The evidence on this point is insufficient

12. All gains are measured spring to spring or winter to winter except for schools in Indiana which are calculated from fall to fall, including fall 2005–2006 for the most recent gains.

to draw any firm conclusions. The data on the not-for-profits is rather scant because few of those organizations have had sufficient history with their schools under current state testing regimes. A number of the not-for-profit firms—e.g., Universal, Foundations, Temple University, the University of Pennsylvania—are also serving non-charter public schools, and separate data on their charter operations was not readily accessible. The not-for-profit operators had only five schools with three years of data in 2005, making it difficult to draw strong conclusions about long-term effects.

What evidence can be adduced suggests there should be no policy issue with the for-profits, relative to the not-for-profits, on student achievement. The average gains for the for-profit managers relative to state gains round to 5, 6, and 8 percentage points for one-, two-, and three-year intervals. The gains for not-for-profits round to 6, 7, and 4 percentage points for one-, two-, and three-year gains, though again the three-year gains are based on too little data to take seriously. Generally speaking, the academic track records of for-profits and not-for-profits are similar and are superior to state averages over the short and longer term. The concern that for-profit managers would trade short-term profits for achievement gains is not supported by the data. The idea that not-for-profits will be academically superior scale operators is also not supported. Both types of scale operators are making gains in excess of state averages. Scale seems to benefit student achievement.

Summary and Recommendations

The funding of public schools in general and of charter schools in particular makes it unlikely that any individual school will have the resources to develop all of the expertise and build all of the systems necessary to maximize its success for students. This point is acknowledged in long-standing arguments for school district consolidation, and should be acknowledged in policy-making for charter schools. Like traditional public schools, charter schools stand to benefit from being part of larger groupings of schools, where pooled resources and economies of scale can produce more support services at a lower cost. Charter policy should allow for these potential benefits.

Policymakers and education experts have no idea what the scale of a school district or a system of schools truly should be. The scale of public school systems—and of public schools—has been determined entirely through political decision-making, constrained by local political geography. Policymakers have never had opportunity to ask: what scale school system would maximize student achievement for a given level of taxpayer commitment? Charter schools offer an unparalleled opportunity for policymakers to let factors other than political influence and tradition determine the scale of public education. Charter schools are driven more by market forces than by political forces—more by choice and competition than by democracy and bureaucracy. Charter schools still need government oversight, for certain. But market forces could and should play a larger role in shaping their development. One force that policymakers could and should leave more to the market is the role of scale organization.

Opponents of charter schools have successfully argued that scale organizations, for-profit and not-for-profit, are a danger to public education. But those arguments were advanced before the evidence to evaluate them was available. Now we know several important things about scale support organizations:

1. Despite the limitations imposed on them by charter school law, scale management organizations are proliferating: they are meeting a need that charter schools are experiencing.

2. Management organizations are not turning into national be-

hemoths threatening the local character of education; they are instead becoming geographically focused, trying to master the local standards, rules, and cultures that distinguish education from state to state.

3. Management organizations are not driving schools to excessive size to increase site efficiencies. Schools working with outside managers are larger than typical charter schools but smaller than traditional public schools. For-profit firms are not driving schools to exceptional size as a rule; even the firms with relatively large schools are still operating close to national norms.
4. For-profit management organizations are moving toward large scale operations at a faster pace than not-for-profit organizations. Though time will tell whether not-for-profits are simply moving more slowly than for-profits because they have different aspirations for scale, none of the organizations examined here has reached a size that would suggest they have reached ideal scale. In all likelihood, whatever their goals at scale, for-profits appear likely to get there faster than not-for-profits.
5. Fears that large size or profits would get in the way of the best interests of students appear unfounded. While schools working with management organizations do not always succeed, and all management organizations do not succeed on average every year, the general tendencies are positive. All management organizations make achievement gains on average. These gains are sometimes only at rates states are making overall. But over the long-term, schools appear to make greater gains with management companies than schools statewide make in general. Finally, though the achievement data on not-for-profits are scant, the data on for-profits are not: schools working with EMOs are gaining at rates increasingly

above state averages the longer schools work with those companies.

Because scale has potential to help charter schools succeed; because there is no evidence that scale organizations, for-profit and not-for-profit, do any harm; and because for-profit scale organizations have potential to reach scale faster than not-for-profit organizations, policymakers should remove the barriers they have erected to scale organizations. Specifically, groups granted charters should be able to operate multiple schools under a single charter. For-profit as well as not-for-profit organizations ought to be able to hold charters and operate charter schools directly. At the very least, not-for-profit charter holders ought to be able to hire for-profit operators to run their schools completely.

6. Chartering and Innovating

Chester E. Finn Jr.

Despite the weighty burdens under which they labor and the many obstacles they encounter, U.S. charter schools have made impressive strides on the innovation front. They've even innovated with respect to the definition of "educational innovation," which is to say many of their notable accomplishments on this front have taken altogether different forms than early charter theorists and backers expected.

That charters would innovate, however, was both expected and promised from the outset, when their proponents made four key claims.

First, these novel schools would provide needed and healthy competition for moribund and monopolistic district public schools and thus force them to change as a result of external pressure.

Second, they would provide quality education options for children who lacked them, especially disadvantaged youngsters unable to afford private schools.

Third, they would offer creative educators, community groups and organizations, entrepreneurs, philanthropists, and others the opportunity to develop and operate their own public schools according to their own educational lights or the needs of the children for whom they are most concerned.

Fourth, these schools would serve as sources of innovation and discovery for American education as a whole, as laboratories or research and development centers, devising new forms of teaching and learning, unique curricula, distinctive ways of organizing schools and novel modes of effectively delivering instruction to children.

It is the last of those promises that I primarily examine here, although, in fact, charter-related innovation has also helped to keep the other three promises and I will note some of the ways.

The problem that the fourth promise sought to solve was embedded in the belief that U.S. education wasn't as good as it needed to be because it had failed to discover effective ways of doing things. It was stuck in a rut and too uniform from one place to another. If only American K–12 education possessed a set of daring "lab schools" to experiment with new and different educational practices (or so this reasoning went), it would make breakthrough discoveries that could then be applied on a mass scale.

Charters, at least to some people, held out the promise that American ingenuity, turned loose to innovate without bureaucratic encumbrance, union strictures and regulatory inhibition, would succeed in transforming education as it had transformed so many other sectors. Call this the Thomas Edison view of schooling. (In 1996, charter pioneer Joe Nathan identified Henry Ford and Apple's Steve Jobs and Steve Wozniak as prototypical designer-inventor-entrepreneurs and models.) Putter about in the lab or workshop, without too many outside constraints, and clever, motivated, imaginative people will invent terrific alternatives to the failed methods of yesteryear. Experiments that worked in charter schools could then be picked up by the "regular system."

"*Without too many outside constraints,*" I said, and that was, of course, a major element of charter-school theology and of the founders' expectations. As other chapters in this volume make clear, reality turned out to be painfully different. Compromise, constraint and a slanted playing field have bedeviled charter schools from the outset, with potentially dire consequences for innovation. Just as families that lack such essentials as bread and milk are unlikely to invent new gourmet taste treats, skimpy funding has made it a challenge for U.S. charter schools to deliver even the basics, even as myriad unwaived rules and laws have pressed these schools to ape rather than deviate from the familiar features and practices of traditional district-operated schools.

Almost from the beginning, critics charged that U.S. charter schools were not, in fact, keeping the innovation promise by coming up with anything truly original, anything that couldn't already be found (if one looked hard enough) in district-operated public schools. Characteristic of this genre, in 2000 Gerald Bracey remarked of charter schools that, "Innovations in the broader sense of the word . . . are rare. In Michigan, for example, evaluators did not find any program or approach that had not already been tried in the public schools."[1]

Are such criticisms valid? Has this promise in fact not been kept? Was it an illusion from the outset? A good idea strangled in its crib? Or was it misunderstood (possibly by those who believed it) and misrepresented by charter critics, perhaps to serve their larger political ends? Have important innovations emerged from charter schools in particular and the charter movement in general? If so, what are they? And what's the likelihood that char-

1. Gerald Bracey, *Charter Schools*, Center for Education Research, Analysis, and Innovation, School of Education, University of Wisconsin-Milwaukee, October 12, 2000.

ter schools will, in the future, serve as a significant fount of innovation?

In a limited and technical sense, the critics have a point. There's practically no imaginable education "program or approach" (to use Bracey's phrase) that cannot already be found somewhere in the vastness of American public education. That goes for good and bad practices alike, things that work and things that don't. American education has much sameness, but it also boasts astonishing diversity—and this was true before charter schools came along.

But that argument misses the point. Innovativeness per se is no virtue if the change represents no improvement. In an era of standards-based reform, in fact, the coin of the education realm is achievement or performance, not sheer novelty or unalloyed differentness. Charter schools, sometimes to their dismay, are being judged more by their success in boosting standardized test scores than by their capacity to generate a parade of inventions and innovations. Some charter people, in fact, feel confined, inhibited, and frustrated by this fact. Yet going where nobody has ever journeyed before is a dreamy ideal that is seldom realized in the 100,000-school expanse of American K–12 education, and isn't all that important, anyway. Indeed, one can argue that the education system's obsession with innovativeness per se is a romantic distraction from the need to take proven practices and known successes and replicate them in more places, deploying them in place of failed approaches and nonfunctional designs. Indeed, even within the charter movement, much of today's smart money is investing not in the invention of yet more models, but in the duplication and propagation of success.

Yet charter schools and the charter movement have made profound and valuable contributions to educational innovation in America—and have done so despite the confined scope, constrained budgets and regulatory shackles that inhibit them. Ten developments on this front deserve note.

First, while cosmopolitans routinely scan the entire national public-education landscape in search of ideas, innovations, examples, and trends, most people are locally oriented. For a particular child, parent, or teacher, public education consists of what's readily accessible where they live. A fine school in Portland doesn't do much for a kid in Tuscaloosa. An innovative pedagogy in the Bronx is of scant value on Arizona's Navaho reservation—and vice versa. What charter schools have been able to do in thousands of places is to distinguish themselves from the pre-existing schools in their vicinities, thus creating what, from the community's standpoint, must fairly be termed innovations and alternatives that didn't otherwise exist. Innovation in situ, we might call it. That charters have done this is acknowledged even by people like Bracey, who grudgingly notes that "some things might be considered an innovation by contrast to the local public school. For instance, if the public schools were emphasizing a whole language approach to the teaching of beginning reading, then a phonics-oriented program might seem innovative to those who adopted it."

Example: Hundreds of "Core Knowledge" schools are scattered about the land, and the concept has been familiar since E. D. Hirsch Jr. coined it more than a decade ago. Core Knowledge curricula can be found in some district schools and private schools, as well as charter schools, and no longer qualify as an innovation per se. But if your family lives in Arvada, Colorado, served by the sprawling Jefferson County school system, the fastest, surest route to a Core Knowledge school for your kids is the Lincoln Academy charter school.[2] Similarly, while single-sex education is scarcely a novelty in the cosmos, if you live in Albany

2. http://lincolnacademy.net.

and want it for your daughter or son, you will gravitate to the only places in town that offer it: the twin "Brighter Choices" charter schools, one for boys and one for girls.[3]

Second, while charter schools may invent few unprecedented practices that cannot be spotted in some district school somewhere, they often mix and match practices in unusual and creative ways. For example, they might be much more instructionally unified than district schools in which teachers can close their doors and ignore what everyone else is teaching. They might be small, personalized, demanding, yet serene. They might include student-initiated learning with close attention to individual youngsters' progress followed by quick remediation when students fall behind. They often engage parents in unusual ways, including "learning contracts," weekly progress bulletins, mandatory parent participation, and suchlike. They may combine instruction with motivation, character development, and moral formation in ways that public schools seldom do. They might have novel staffing patterns. They might be conventional about instruction but join it to health, recreation, and social services. Such blends of instructional practices, school climate and organization, staffing and leadership, and ancillary activities are rare in public education, precisely because union contracts, school board policies, and bureaucratic boundaries work against them. Thus, when one seeks innovativeness in charter schools, it's not individual practices so much as packages, combinations, and connections among them that hold the greatest promise for children, families, and educators—and for those seeking to replicate success.

Example: New York City's Harlem-based "Village Academies," the first of which began in 2003, are remarkable meldings of school features tailored to the schools' missions and their inner-city, early-adolescent clienteles. These features were carefully re-

3. http://www.brighterchoice.org.

searched and meticulously assembled by school founder Deborah Kenny.[4] Thus the schools combine a liberal arts curriculum with extra attention to reading and math skills; they have a nine-hour school day and 200-day year; they're organized into "small learning villages" that strive to individualize attention to students; and they commence college counseling in sixth grade.

Third, for a nontrivial number of public-school systems, the chartering mechanism, constrained as it is, has allowed them to try things they couldn't easily do within their own even-more-confining bureaucratic rules and contractual restrictions. "Pro-active chartering," we can call it. Whether it's networks of start-up schools in big cities like Chicago, New York, or Philadelphia, unusual school alternatives in the Minnesota towns of Northfield, Waseca, and Faribault, Houston's "Accelerated Learning and Transition Academy," the Los Angeles campus of "High Tech High," or virtual charter schools in a number of Ohio districts, some reform-minded superintendents and school boards have seized on the charter option as a way to test or demonstrate changes that they know make sense but are otherwise powerless to effect. Unfortunately, many other superintendents lack the vision or political will to do this—but in those situations it's not unheard of for other community leaders to seize upon the charter mechanism to inject quality and options into the city's education offerings, as Indianapolis mayor Bart Peterson and Oakland mayor Jerry Brown have done.

Example: Chicago's "ACE Tech High School"—ACE stands for "architecture, construction, engineering"—was created as a charter school because local building trades firms and unions had long had great difficulty working with the school system's vocational education department, and because it was crucial that skilled union tradespeople who were not state-certified as teach-

4. http://www.villageacademies.org.

ers be able to instruct its students.[5] A knowledgeable observer of the Chicago scene remarks that this school's creation "caused an interesting and even amusing level of stress within the local labor movement as one branch of labor created a school in order to do a better job than another branch. The teachers union was not happy but the building trades couldn't have cared less."

In Colorado, where, until recently, districts have been the only charter authorizers—and many proved grudging in this role—several superintendents recognized that the charter law could be deployed for the district's own purposes. Denver, Montrose, and Strasburg, for example, launched charter schools to provide alternative programs for high-risk students and/or "recovery" programs for dropouts.

Fourth, any number of promising schools might not have happened at all, and certainly wouldn't have spread, but for the charter option. Prominent examples include Core Knowledge, KIPP, The Met, High Tech High, Aspire Public Schools, National Heritage Academies, and Edison Schools. "Virtual" schooling would not have reached nearly as many youngsters in nearly as many states were it not for the invention of "virtual charter schools," such as the networks run by Connections Academy and K12.[6] Though successful replication of good schools remains a huge challenge for public education in general, the fact is that these schools are different enough, sometimes controversial enough, and often in need of such unconventional resources (people, budgets, calendars, schedules, materials, etc.), that chartering enabled them to thrive and spread in ways that district governance only occasionally allows. We can contrast this with the tale of "New American Schools" in the early 90s, which devised some interesting (and some banal) school designs but relied on states

5. http://www.acetechnical.org/index.htm.
6. http://www.connectionsacademy.com and www.k12.com.

and districts to embrace and implement comprehensive change models. By comparison, chartering fosters the spread of these other models today.

Interestingly, the "scaling" of charter-led innovation is not occurring within the district-school system so much as via the spread of successful charter models through the fascinating new entities known as Education Management Organizations (EMO's) and Charter Management Organizations (CMO's). (The former are profit-seeking firms such as Edison, Mosaica, White Hat and National Heritage Academies. The latter are non-profit organizations.) Virtual or shadow school systems—systems that replicate and refine successful models first developed as one-off schools—are arising via these enterprises, sometimes across a state or region, sometimes across the nation.

Though such models are common in the business sector, U.S. school systems have traditionally been geographically defined. We are now discovering via charters, CMO's, EMO's and kindred enterprises, that a single entity can successfully operate similar schools in many communities scattered across the landscape. The management arrangements differ but the implications are profound, not just for school organization, administration and delivery but also for the appearance of what can fairly be termed "brand name schools" that may one day be as ubiquitous as Holiday Inns, Toyota dealerships and Olive Garden restaurants.

Organizations pushing hard for large-scale school reform, such as the Bill and Melinda Gates Foundation, have discovered to their dismay that, except in rare circumstances where the political and leadership stars are well aligned at the top of a school system, changing existing district schools—particularly in big cities—is excruciatingly difficult. They're finding it faster and more productive to launch new schools. That, in turn, attracts them to the charter option and to CMO's, EMO's, and other means of taking charter-devised innovation to scale.

Example: The Knowledge Is Power Program (KIPP) schools began as charters and most of them (forty-two of forty-eight at present) remain charters, though there's no fast rule that they must be. But because they expect so much of their teachers—ultra-long days, weeks and years, plus 24/7 cell phone accessibility—it's exceptionally difficult to work this out within the bounds of a conventional salary schedule, state certification rules, and union contracts. Additionally, the KIPP curriculum, while tailored to a state's academic standards (and often blowing the lid off local test scores), is distinctive and not well suited to a district's standard offerings. Moreover, one of the "five pillars" of KIPP is that the school must be a "school of choice," which is usually much easier to secure under the rules of a charter law than under the constraints of a district's attendance zones and bus routes. The KIPP organization is not, strictly speaking, a CMO. It's more like a leadership training, school development, and franchising operation—yet another organizational innovation spawned by the charter world.[7]

Fifth, though districts may not embrace different practices because they were piloted by charter schools, pressure from charter-induced competition has prodded a number of districts to innovate with their regular schools, if only to stanch the pupil hemorrhage and appeal more directly to parents who suddenly have viable alternatives for their daughters and sons. A 2001 federal study of "ripple effects" found every school system in a five-state sample making changes in "business and/or operations in response to charter schools. In 90 percent of those districts, leaders indicated they made changes in multiple areas of their district's operations in response to charter schools." [8] Other studies are more

7. http://www.kipp.org/kippschools.

8. Gregg Vanourek, *State of the Charter Movement 2005*, National Association of Public Charter Schools, http://www.charterschoolleadershipcouncil.org/pdf/sotm2005.pdf, page 24.

skeptical about the extent to which district schools have changed their practices in response to charter-driven competition, but everyone in the charter movement has anecdotes that suggest this is occurring.

Examples: The Ohio landscape is figuratively strewn with "virtual" schools started by districts in reaction to the thousands of students who have exited in favor of statewide virtual charter schools (and because districts spotted the availability of federal and state start-up dollars for such initiatives). Minnesota's Forest Lake district started a Montessori school of its own after parents sought to launch a charter school in the Montessori mode.

A decade ago, one of America's sagest school superintendents, Boston's Tom Payzant, in collaboration with that city's teacher union, initiated a network of semi-autonomous "pilot" schools, now numbering seventeen such.[9] Here is how the Boston Foundation and Payzant explained them in 2002:

> Pilot schools resulted from an agreement among the Boston Teachers Union (BTU), the Boston School Committee and the Mayor, which was incorporated into the 1994 collective bargaining agreement between the BTU and the Boston Public Schools. Pilot schools were created, in part, as a direct response to the competition posed by charter schools. . . . Dr. Thomas Payzant, Superintendent of Boston Public Schools, welcomed the Foundation's support for encouraging the conversion of existing schools, saying, "Pilot schools are a critical part of the Boston Public Schools' reform agenda. They were conceived by the district and the union working together. Parents want their children to attend, the results are impressive, and they keep the district competitive. Now, it is important to encourage more Boston public schools to seek pilot status."[10]

Unfortunately, the Boston venture also shows how vulnerable

9. http://www.ccebos.org/pilotschools/schools.html.
10. http://www.tbf.org/About/about-L2.asp?ID=97.

such innovations are to shifts in the political winds. When the local teachers union acquired a new president in June 2003 (for the first time in twenty-eight years), he turned out to be a critic of the pilot-school program, objecting, in particular, to the schools' freedom to set their own teachers' hours and calendars and to decide how and whether additional "stipends" would be paid to those who work longer. "Forced overtime," union president Richard Stutman termed it, as he sought to curb the schools' autonomy in personnel matters—and to extract more salary dollars from the school system. The result, in mid-2005, was termed by *Education Week* "an increasingly bitter standoff" between union and district that, among its consequences, is preventing at least one more elementary school from joining the pilot network, even though its teachers voted (two years ago) to do so.

Sixth, charters have, as intended, created havens for disadvantaged youngsters in need of decent alternatives to bad district schools and unable to afford private schools. From the children's standpoint, at least, that amounts to a major innovation. Although Milton Friedman, father of the voucher movement, terms charters "a halfway solution," and although not every charter school is a good school, the waiting lists at many attest to their popularity and the demand for more of them. The Charter School Leadership Council estimates that, if there were enough charter schools today to accommodate all the girls and boys on waiting lists—20,000 in California, 15,000 in Massachusetts, etc.—total charter enrollments would be 20 percent greater and some 700 more schools (at their present average size) would be needed. The reason demand outstrips supply is, of course, the many caps, constraints, and obstacles that block the creation and expansion of charter schooling in nearly every state.

The overwhelming majority of today's 3,400 charter schools are located within the borders of troubled urban school systems large and small, and most of their million pupils are poor and minority. Vanourek says that in 2002–2003, 58.6 percent of charter students were minority and 35 percent were eligible for subsidized federal lunches (and there's reason to suspect undercounting). Moreover, a large fraction of charter schools specifically seek to serve pupil populations that are needy in other ways. A 2003 survey reported that "28 percent of charter schools target low-income students or dropouts, 27 percent identify gifted and talented students as a target population to be served, nearly a quarter target English as a Second Language (ESL) students, 18 percent view teen parents as a focus, 12 percent specifically seek disabled students, 11 percent target court-adjudicated youth, and 10 percent target expelled youth."[11]

Examples: Within four years of its founding, Washington's KIPP "Key Academy" was the highest-scoring middle school in the District of Columbia. Its cousin in the Bronx, one of the nation's two original KIPP schools, has for eight straight years been ranked the highest performing middle school in that impoverished borough.

The W.E.B. DuBois Academy, one of Ohio's highest-performing charter schools, now styles itself the "best school in Cincinnati," a claim that nobody in the Queen City seems to dispute.

The Chicago Charter School Foundation (CCSF) operates seven campuses serving some 4500 Windy City youngsters. Demand for places in these schools greatly exceeds capacity. In the summer of 2004, for example, 1700 more youngsters applied than could be accommodated—illustrative of the desperation felt by many Chicago families to find better education options for their children than the district itself provides. This abundance of applicants, and the fact that CCSF uses a randomized lottery to determine which applicants will attend its schools, means that it's also an excellent place for careful research, which was undertaken

11. Vanourek, page 12.

by Harvard economist and Koret Task Force member Caroline M. Hoxby. She and a colleague report that CCSF students (who entered between kindergarten and fifth grade), after spending an average of two years in their charter schools, score, on average, six percentile points higher than similar youngsters who were "lotteried out" and remained in the regular district-school system.

Seventh, chartering has become an option—not necessarily a good one—for transforming dysfunctional schools in the era of standards-based accountability. The basic charter "bargain"—greater operational freedom in return for stronger academic results, with the school's very continuation dependent on its success in delivering those results—meshes well with standards-based reform. Congress and several states now see "chartering" as a way of reconstituting faltering district schools.

State (or district-initiated) interventions into poorly performing schools can take the form of chartering them, reconstituting them as charters, or closing them down and replacing them with start-up charters, perhaps operating in the same building. Some versions of reconstitution-via-charter are causing heartburn among charter aficionados who contend that the people associated with a school have to *want* it to be a charter school for that approach to have a decent chance of succeeding, i.e. that "involuntary charter school" is an oxymoron. Still, if the reconstitution is thorough enough, such as emptying out the building and in effect starting a new school in the old structure, it may succeed as a charter school. Colorado has pioneered a version of this with its own state accountability law, which provides that after several years of low performance by a district school, the state will issue a "request for proposals," inviting outside groups to propose converting that school to a charter. For various reasons, little has yet occurred under this provision, but in early 2005, with KIPP's help, the Denver Public Schools "reconstituted" the chronically low-performing Cole Middle School as a charter to be known as "KIPP: Cole College Prep."

California has a similar provision on the books. As one option for a chronically low-performing school, parents may petition the state to convert the school into a charter. Nobody has done this yet, but the Sacramento school system engaged in a version of it in 2003 when, rather than face a state takeover, it closed the venerable Sacramento High School and reopened it as a charter school run by a non-profit group called St. Hope Public Schools. (By all accounts, the school is thriving under its new structure.)

Much more of this sort of thing may be on the horizon courtesy of No Child Left Behind, which prescribes, among the options afforded districts for transforming low-performing schools in "corrective action" (and that have proven resistant to improvement via milder interventions), that "re-opening the school as a public charter school" is now a federally-sanctioned intervention strategy. How this will work is anybody's guess.[12]

Eighth, the charter movement is drawing new people into public education—and keeping them there longer than the traditional system could. This is palpable at the annual "summit" sponsored by the New Schools Venture Fund, where hundreds of education innovators (and some profiteers and hangers-on) throng a hotel lobby and corridors, gossiping, exchanging business cards, exploring deals, commiserating about political and bureaucratic obstacles, and talking about curriculum, teachers, technology, and test scores.

One cannot help but contrast that scene with standard-issue education conferences, where real innovativeness is in short supply, resentment of change is the norm, and the best-loved speakers are those who rationalize the current performance of U.S.

12. See http://www.ecs.org/clearinghouse/54/25/5425.htm for additional information.

schools and decry the scoundrels who aver that the nation is in jeopardy.

Attendees at the "New Schools" confabs also appear younger, keener and leaner, less fixated on the next cocktail hour or exhibitor break.

Example: The SEED Foundation is a non-profit group in Washington D.C. that runs the country's best-known college-oriented charter *boarding* school, designed for disadvantaged teenagers from such troubled circumstances that going home after school each day is not wise.[13] It's becoming a model for other communities, even as it does an exemplary job of meeting the educational needs of several hundred D.C. youngsters. The two impressive young men who founded and still lead the school— one with an MBA in finance from Wharton Business School, the other a trustee of Princeton— wouldn't likely be found working within the public-education system absent the charter opportunity. Nor have they lost their sense of enterprise. If all goes well, Baltimore will soon be home to the second SEED academy.

Ninth, though charter schools should not base their reputation for innovativeness on pure novelty or invention, some have characteristics so distinctive as to be genuinely difficult to find in traditional district schools. These include grade configurations that are rare in public school systems, such as schools spanning grades 6–12 and K–12 on a single site, easing or eliminating damaging transitions for kids and giving parents the option of circumventing the middle school entirely. They also include imaginative dropout-recovery schools that enable students to earn money while learning both technical and academic skills. (See, for example, Dayton's ISUS and Mound Street charter schools.)[14]

13. http://www.seedfoundation.com/SEEDfoundation/SEEDSITE/Program_overview.htm.

14. Learn more about these schools at http://www.cew.wisc.edu/charterSchools/profileISUS.asp and http://www.moundstreet.k12.oh.us/moundstreeta/site/default.asp.

Minnesota's statutory requirement that teachers comprise a majority of each charter school governing board, though placed in the law to placate the teacher unions, has actually given rise to some unusual administrative arrangements. The EdVisions "co-operative" believes strongly in "teacher ownership" of its ten affiliated charter schools, pivoting off a design pioneered at the Minnesota New Country School, a rural school that has no principal and is led by a team of teachers.

Others have used chartering as a way to solve structural or governance problems that once plagued them. For example, several rural communities in Colorado—Marble, Guffey, Dinosaur, Paradox and others—were aggrieved because district consolidation had erased their sense of local control of their public schools—something especially important in tiny towns where the school is often the center of community life. District headquarters might be as much as fifty miles away, literally on the other side of the mountains, and they may subscribe to very different cultures and values than do those in the schools they govern. The charter law, in effect, enabled the rural communities to "secede" from these sprawling districts and recapture community ownership. What's unique here is not what goes on inside the school. What's unique is a functional governance arrangement that is well-tailored to a community's circumstances but otherwise unattainable within the ever-larger structures that dominate American public education.

Tenth and finally, chartering as a concept is beginning to creep into a few other domains.[15] Ohio has developed a modest program of "charter colleges of education" that prepare candidates for "alternative certification" and California State University at Los Angeles boasts a "charter college of education."

15. Some analysts say it was widespread in many other domains long before it percolated into public education and that, in fact, innovation is seeping the other direction.

Virginia's legislature came close to "chartering" that state's public universities and conferring greater autonomy on them; in 2005 lawmakers agreed to a plan whereby (without using the charter label) interested campuses can approximate that status.

Major changes in Colorado's public higher education system in the past few years were modeled on charter-school governance, with individual campuses getting many state regulations waived in return for negotiated "performance contracts."

Iowa now calls six of its state agencies (e.g. child welfare, corrections) "charter agencies" and exempts them from many bureaucratic rules and routines in return for fiscal savings and measurable consumer benefits.

The word "charter" isn't the crucial element. What's distinctive is the shift from large bureaucratic structures, uniformity, and command-and-control governance to something more like a contractual arrangement between the public and a provider of public services. Charter sponsorship, as explained in chapter 4 in this volume, is akin to outsourcing the provision of those services rather than their exclusive delivery via government agencies and government employees. This is becoming more and more widespread in myriad domains within and outside of education.

That's ten, and to my eye they add up to plenty of important innovating. On balance, it can fairly be said that, while there may be few things that a given charter school is doing that a district somewhere isn't also doing, the American charter experience is, in fact, yielding an immense amount of desirable innovation on multiple fronts. It's doing so, moreover, in spite of the myriad constraints upon it. Perhaps adversity begets creativity—or in the more familiar phrasing, necessity is the mother of invention. But one should also try to imagine what more might have been accomplished on the innovation front if the playing field weren't so steeply tilted against the charter venture.

That's not to say that all such schools are succeeding or that the charter experiment is a slam-dunk success. Indeed, we've also learned over these fifteen years that putting the charter label on a school doesn't make it a good one. But charter schools that are really bad have closed down, hundreds of them, albeit not enough yet (good sponsorship remains a work in progress), which is more than one can say for district schools. Thus, chartering is also an important, if not yet fully successful, innovation on the accountability front, which is particularly important in an era of standards-based reform.

What does the future hold? Most importantly, I believe, we can glimpse the emergence of a new model for organizing and governing public education—and for creating new or different schools. Ted Kolderie calls it public education's "open sector," the part that's free from traditional geographic boundaries and district bureaucracies, the part that allows for invention and innovation. But it's even more than that. The organizational changes we're witnessing suggest that charter schools may themselves be taken to scale—and that the results-based and always contingent relationship between a charter school and its sponsor might even become the norm rather than the exception in American public education. That would be one heck of an innovation.

What will keep that from happening? Self-destructive forces within the charter movement will contribute but the successful spread of this promising innovation will be blocked, above all, by the intense political opposition of those who are now pressing hard to contain it; who want to burden it with even more shackles; and who absolutely, positively don't want it to spread. Don't believe them, though, when they cite charters' alleged lack of innovation as a reason why it shouldn't.

7. Realizing Chartering's Full Potential

Paul T. Hill

Many people who supported charter schools from the beginning did so because of what they could envision developing in the long run. They could imagine a big city like Chicago or Cleveland having an education system very much like the marketplace for independent schools in a wealthy city like San Francisco or Seattle. In a city with a mature charter school sector:

- Families would have many options and schools' specialties, strengths, and weaknesses would be well known so that parents know what they are choosing; moreover many options would be available to the poor, not just the well off;
- Information would be plentiful about what individual schools do well and badly, and how all schools perform on common outcome measures;
- Except for the newest entrants, all schools would have clear track records so both parents and public oversight bodies can consider long term outcomes like graduation rates, student performance at the next level of education, college attendance

and graduation, and employment success as well as short term outcomes like test scores;

- Teachers could select the schools that best match their interests, that most need their individual skills, and that are willing and able to pay for classroom excellence;
- New teachers and individuals with rare skills could compete for jobs and be paid for the value of their contribution to the school, not just for their seniority or degrees attained;
- Many teachers and administrators would have experience working in schools of choice and understand the importance of collaboration, sharing responsibility, and paying close attention to parents;
- Organizations that run schools, though varied in their approach to instruction, would all have strong incentives to invest in good instruction and work hard to maintain quality;
- Schools that had bad performance records or lose the confidence of parents will be unable to remain open;
- There would always be room for a school with a powerful new idea—including new uses of time, place, and technology—or a way to meet a previously unmet need;
- Business and financial institutions would understand schools and compete to supply them with everything from loans and insurance to facilities, maintenance, and supplies.

Paul E. Peterson's chapter shows that local marketplaces can develop in this way under the right combination of circumstances. No one thought such a situation would emerge overnight. The behemoth of bureaucratic-style public school "systems" was too well entrenched and politically powerful. The alternative would develop gradually, as the first charter schools developed loyal clienteles and attracted more applicants than they could admit, and created a demand for additional charters. As the number of schools grew, so would the number of parents who expected to send their children to charter schools and the numbers of teachers and parents who had charter schools experience and knew how to work effectively within them. Companies and financial institutions, at first unfamiliar with charter schools, would develop lines of business to serve them. School districts, facing competition for students from nimbler and more efficient schools, would seek to compete by devolving important decisions about spending and staffing to the building level and cutting back their central office overhead. Ultimately, all schools would compete on the same basis and the reinvented district would be as aggressive about pursuing new ideas and seeking replacements for low performing schools as were the charter schools. Innovations like those described by Chester E. Finn Jr. would become widespread, and the whole public education system would always be open to new ideas.

The situation described above can emerge only if the charter sector grows steadily over time and large numbers of schools develop into well-defined educational options. Today, newness and small scale are themselves barriers to the success of charter schools. Civic and educational leaders who hope chartering will attain the broad vision sketched above need to make sure the movement survives long enough for its schools to develop track records for quality instruction. But a few good schools are not enough. A large-scale alternative can only emerge once people can actually visualize how it would work in practice, not just in theory. Chartering needs the running room to function as a bona fide demonstration of "different."

Looked upon from the future, today's charter schools will be seen as pioneers that fought their way uphill and gradually developed a marketplace of real options. Though many good things have happened in the charter school movement, it is still a very long way from realizing this vision. This is true in part because starting good schools and building a track record can't happen overnight; it takes years, more than the charter school movement has had to date. Another and probably more important reason is that opponents of charter schools have understood the long-term vision perfectly and have worked to prevent it by tilting the playing field against charter schools.

When the first charter-school laws were enacted, nobody wanted to dwell on how bad a deal they offered. It was clear that people who wanted to run charter schools had to take on all the risks of a new small business, engage in a school start-up process about which little was known, and compete for students and teachers against district-run public schools that were better funded and well established. It was clear they would get less money than the district-run schools with which they had to compete, but as Eric Osberg shows, nobody knew just how big the funding gap would be. Caroline M. Hoxby shows how effective legislative provisions were in tilting the playing field against charter schools. As Chester E. Finn Jr. and Paul T. Hill show, when charter laws were first enacted nobody anticipated how carelessly government would play its role in approving and overseeing charter schools. Nor did charter supporters, optimists all, anticipate how relentlessly opponents, particularly teachers' unions and school boards, would work to make new problems for charter schools and exacerbate the existing ones.

Opponents' tactics have also prevented natural development of the charter sector—not only the schools themselves but the suppliers of goods, services, and financing that schools need, and the teacher and administrator human resource pools that inevitably emerge when a kind of school has operated in many places over a long time.

The human resource issue is particularly important: it is why well established genres of private school—e.g., Yeshivas, Montessori, Quaker, Jesuit and Jewish Day schools—can be reproduced successfully in many places with relatively little infrastructure. In any large city, there are people who have attended such schools and perhaps even taught in them. People starting a new school of these types face many challenges, but they can start with a group of teachers and administrators who share many principles and experiences, whether or not they know one another personally.

The first few charter schools starting in a community have no such advantages. They must instead hire people who have never worked in such a school before. Not only will new teachers and administrators have disparate ideas about teaching and collaboration, but they will also lack experience working in a school that must attract students in order to survive and must live strictly within its income. With time, the charter school human resource pool should grow, and future charter schools should have less difficulty finding the people they need. However, the human resource pool will never become strong if the number of charter schools in a community can be kept low and existing schools are constantly forced to fight for their lives. As several chapters in this book show, school boards and teachers' unions, while complaining about charter schools' supposed advantages, have worked to de-stabilize schools, made sure they had less money than other public schools, and discouraged experienced teachers from joining them.

The charter movement overall has survived a hostile environment and even thrived in some places. Individual schools have fallen victim to one problem or another, but many schools have defined themselves, developed stable staffs and loyal followings, and offered learning opportunities not otherwise available.

Some entrepreneurs have also innovated in response to adversity, compensating for the absence of local suppliers and human resource pools by creating multi-site school providers, called charter management organizations (CMOs) or, in the case of for-profit firms, education management organizations (EMOs). Despite the many barriers to for-profits' success documented above by John E. Chubb, EMOs have become important elements of the charter movement. Like networks of private schools, they provide the staff recruitment and training, legal and financial services, and legal representation needed by groups of charter schools. Such organizations can help level the playing field by making up for the lack of charter school support infrastructure in a given locality. However, for the charter school movement overall to reap all the advantages of large scale, it will also need local marketplaces for charter-related services and human resource pools that are, relative to vertically integrated CMOs and EMOs, more flexible, more open to new ideas, and less expensive to build and maintain.

In addition to adapting to harsh environments, chartering has also won new friends, especially among the superintendents and school boards of some of America's largest cities, who found that the school systems they inherited are simply unable to meet the higher academic standards set by state and federal governments. For similar reasons, a growing pro-choice movement among African Americans and Hispanics has also strengthened pro-charter coalitions in many places.

Yet the opponents work continually to tilt the playing field even more steeply against charter schools. It is not clear, for example, how much more the movement can grow if state legislatures stick with existing caps on school numbers, or if funding arrangements and government authorizers' duties are not made fairer and more neutral. To date, charter schools have defeated most efforts to unionize their teachers, but proposed legislative changes that would create a bias toward unionization and coverage by district collective bargaining agreements could cripple charter schools.

It is also clear that the charter movement can grow and improve significantly only if the large foundations continue to support it. Though many schools are learning to operate on enrollment-based funding, most charter schools need other money for the one-time costs of start-up and facilities purchase. Though a few individuals will donate years of their time and spend their own money on start-up, lack of financial support will prevent many capable people from starting charter schools.

Ultimately, charter schools will be recognized as a public responsibility, and states and localities will create tax-supported venture capital pools for charter start-up. But for now, any hope that charter schools will become much more numerous—enough to provide options for all the poor and minority families that want them and to create the needed local services infrastructure and human resource pools—depends heavily on private investment.

Despite opponents' efforts to tilt the playing field against charter schools, charter schools have many advantages over schools run by politically controlled bureaucracies. These advantages include discretion over use of funds, ability to use time, money, and instructional technologies in innovative ways, freedom to hire teachers and to compete for people of high ability by offering attractive packages of working conditions and pay. They also have access to philanthropic investment and to private risk capital.

However, a profoundly hostile regulatory environment makes it difficult for schools to exploit these advantages. Highly capable organizations are less likely to try providing schools if the field is tilted against them. Because so many obstacles are rooted in public policy, or in the lack of market provision of key goods and services, individual schools cannot overcome them. Overcoming supply side barriers requires concerted action by pro-choice policy activists, philanthropists, businesses, and school heads.

Barriers to Chartering and How They Can Be Overcome

The most important barriers to charter school development are state, legal, and policy frameworks including poorly crafted charter laws (analyzed above by Caroline M. Hoxby),[1] inequitable funding (Osberg), and inadequate authorizers (Finn Jr. and Hill). There are two additional barriers—first, an underdeveloped infrastructure of people and organizations able to provide services charter schools need; and second, school districts' reluctance to use the chartering provisions of No Child Left Behind. This section will define the problems posed by each of these barriers and suggest how they can be overcome.

State Legal and Policy Frameworks

Charter School Laws

Caps on the numbers of schools can prevent groups with sound ideas from opening charter schools, and can prevent the charter sector in any locality from gaining the advantages of large scale. This in turn denies families access to a real marketplace of viable options. Fixed limits on charter terms, often three to five years with no clear criteria for renewal, can force charter schools to fight for their lives just as staff and families have learned how to work together effectively. Term limits also put all charter schools, even highly effective ones, at risk of politically motivated non-

1. Hoxby's results are broader than those of an earlier study on one feature of state laws. For evidence that laws allowing multiple charter authorizers lead increased numbers of charter schools see Jack Buckley and Simona Kuscova, *The Effects of Institutional Variation on Policy Outcomes: The Case of Charter Schools in the States*, New York, National Center for Research on Privatization in Education, Occasional Paper 79, 2003.

renewal. Each can discourage some capable entrepreneurs from starting schools.

The same provisions can discourage financial institutions from developing lines of business, lending money to charter schools, insuring them, and providing goods and services that district-run public schools get from their central offices but that charter schools need to buy.

As John E. Chubb argues above, charter law provisions that bar for-profit firms from receiving charters and groups holding a charter from operating multiple schools also cut off important sources of entrepreneurship and private investment.

Finally, state laws can limit schools' freedom of action by requiring them to hire only certified teachers. This can cut off charter schools' access to artists, musicians, and mathematicians and scientists who are not certified teachers. It can also force charter schools to hire teachers in a labor market where wages have been artificially inflated by restrictions on supply, and discourage experimentation with technology-rich instructional methods that require new kinds of teachers. Federal law also interferes with charter schools' access to good teachers, via the NCLB "highly qualified teacher" requirement. Because this rule has been interpreted to favor education-school-trained teachers, it limits charter schools' ability to make innovative use of artists, scientists, mathematicians, and other masters of key subject matter.

Pro-charter people shouldn't kid themselves that the movement can live with these provisions. They are, as intended, strong barriers against the emergence of a healthy charter sector. The remedies are clear enough. Charter laws need to be amended to:

- Empower new authorizers, including colleges and universities, mayors, and qualified nonprofits in states where school boards hold a monopoly on authorizing charter schools.
- Protect charter schools from arbitrary denial of applications

by establishing appeal processes, to a state agency or independent body, in each state.

- Eliminate arbitrary caps on the numbers of charter schools. Amend state laws so that the number of charter schools depends only on the availability of competent and willing school providers.
- Eliminate fixed terms for charter schools, in favor of provisions that make it clear a school's charter is valid only as long as it can demonstrate student learning.
- Eliminate bans on for-profit firms holding charters directly, in favor of common funding and oversight provisions for all charter schools, no matter who runs them.
- Allow an organization holding one charter to operate multiple schools as long as all their schools meet agreed performance expectations.
- Allow charter schools to employ teachers and administrators in whatever numbers, and with whatever mixtures of skill and experience necessary to deliver the school's instructional program. All authorizers have ample power to reject a charter proposal in which the staffing plan does not match the instructional methods to be used.

Charter school associations are pursuing this legislative agenda in a few states, but in most states charter school supporters have no agenda other than defending what little they have. This needs to become a multi-state agenda with designated initiative leaders and agendas in each state.

A model for the kind of multi-state legislative campaign required is the national Business Roundtable's standards-based reform initiative, which the organization pursued in the early 1990s. After creating a common nationwide legislative agenda, the Roundtable designated leadership groups in every state to press governors and key legislators to enact it. The national Roundtable provided materials and assistance to designees in every state, and produced an annual state-by-state progress report. The result was a much more concerted, and ultimately effective, legislative strategy than any one state business group would have pursued on its own.

The national business community has not stepped up on charter schools, preferring less controversial if less effective reforms. However, others can imitate their tactics. A similar foundation-backed effort, managed by the national Alliance of Public Charter Schools, could be effective.

Inequitable Funding for Charter Students

The school financing provisions of charter-school laws also impede the movement's development. These include funding schemes that give charter schools only a fraction of the per pupil amount available to public school districts, and exclusion of charter schools from valuable things that district-run schools get free, including facilities and state contributions to teacher pensions.

As Eric Osberg's chapter shows, compared to public school districts, charter schools get less money for every pupil they educate. Compared to individual public schools, charters also must pay for many things that their competitors get free—everything from facilities to accounting services, insurance, teacher pensions, and often special education services. True, charter schools often have sources of income that district-run public schools don't, including federal start-up funds and philanthropic contributions, but these are trivial compared to regular public schools' much greater access to federal program funds and to hidden support provided by state government. States (e.g. Illinois) support school districts by subsidizing teacher pensions and other benefits for which charter schools must pay market rates.

Public school financing is such a mess that not even school district CFOs know how much money they have or how it is distributed.[2] Though most charter schools are independent of districts, they suffer from districts' financial chaos. Muddled accounting and uncontrolled spending cost money. Districts, having wasted money that could be spent on instruction in their own schools, resist any further financial drains, even when they are relieved of the obligation of educating the children for which money was provided them. Districts therefore join teachers' unions in pressing for charter funding arrangements that provide less money per pupil than the districts themselves get. In these ways, opponents work to force charter schools to help pay for districts' inefficiency.

Charter schools would clearly benefit from a more transparent method of funding public education—one that accounted for state and local funds on a per pupil basis.[3] Compared to the current funding practices, which focus money on programs, buildings, and job slots rather than the children to be educated, pupil-based funding would be easy to track. Money could also be quickly reassigned from one school to another when families exercise choice. Extra money could be allocated to children who pose particular educational challenges—non-English speaking immigrants, the poor, and the disabled. A pupil-based funding system would guarantee that the same amount would be spent on a child no matter where he or she went to school. It would also ensure that charter schools got all the money taxpayers contributed for the education of their children.

2. See Marguerite Roza and Paul T. Hill, "How Can Anyone Say What's Adequate If Nobody Knows How Money Is Spent Now?" in *Courting Failure: How School Finance Lawsuits Exploit Judges' Good Intentions and Harm Our Children*, Education Next Book, ed. Eric Hanushek (Stanford, CA: Hoover Institution Press, forthcoming 2006).

3. See Thomas B. Fordham Institute, *Fund the Child: Tackling Inequity and Antiquity in School Finance* (Washington, D.C.: June 2006).

Chartering can benefit from a rationalization of public-school finance, but supporters should understand that not all forms of rationalization are equally good. Supporters of school finance "adequacy" lawsuits would increase total public funding without changing the way money is allocated and controlled.[4] Charter schools might get a little more money as a result of adequacy litigation, but school districts and the schools they run would get much more, thus worsening charters' competitive position.

Charter supporters need to campaign for pupil-based funding at least as vigorously as they do for removal of unproductive regulations and arbitrary caps on the numbers of schools. They need to risk losing the support of those who favor school choice only because they think it will cost less.

Too Many Inept or Hostile Charter Authorizers

Many state laws allow only local school boards to charter schools. This creates a fox-in-the-henhouse situation, in which the very institutions that have the most to fear from the development of a vibrant charter sector are able to block its development. As Finn Jr. and Hill note, only a tiny fraction of the number of local school boards legally empowered to authorize charter schools have approved even one charter school. Even when local school boards approve charters, they are much more likely than other authorizers to sponsor conversion schools, essentially existing public schools that do not bring new providers into public education or fuel development of new services.

In many places, charter schools are handicapped by the authorizers' incapacity or hostility. Charter schools don't benefit from having weak or negative authorizers. To the contrary, authorizers that approve charters and then ignore them can turn

4. See the companion Koret Task Force book being published in the same month as this one, Eric Hanushek, ed., *Courting Failure*.

nasty and arbitrary when a problem occurs and they are charged with neglect. Authorizer unpredictability is a serious entry barrier for potentially competent charter school operators and for potential providers of services and financing. Hostile authorizers kill the very entities they are supposed to protect.

From the enactment of the first charter laws, government agencies were clearly assigned responsibility for charter approval and oversight. This is sensible in principle; if charters are "public" schools there has to be some plausible chain of responsibility that traces to the public. Reasonable observers would expect these agencies to hire the people and create the systems necessary for government to oversee independent providers. After all, government has been contracting out for goods and services for decades, and many local, federal, and state agencies have learned that good performance by providers requires smart proposal evaluation, clear contracts, and knowledgeable oversight.[5]

But school districts, the one entity designated by every state law to authorize charter schools, generally did not want to take on the function at all. Most made no arrangements for soliciting and evaluating proposals, and many that felt forced to consider charter schools often assigned responsibility to central office units that had many other tasks. Chartering was often last minute, ad hoc, and inconsistent. In states where there was no appeal to district decisions, many authorizers turn down charter applications without considering the merits of particular applications.

Other authorizers, particularly state departments of education and state colleges and universities, have taken their jobs much more seriously, developing the kinds of in-house expertise and data systems that government has always needed to oversee public health services or weapons systems development.

5. See Frank Camm, "Strategic Sourcing in the Air Force," in *Strategic Appraisal: United States Air and Space Power in the 21st Century*, ed. Zalmay Khalilzad and Jeremy Shapiro, MR-1314-AF, RAND, 2002, pp. 397–435.

As school districts awaken to the need to charter schools—in order to meet parents' demands and provide the NCLB-required options for children in consistently low-performing schools—they will need to become competent authorizers. They can get some help from the foundation-funded National Association of Charter School Authorizers. However, even the best charter authorizers are short on funding and capacity, and are just starting to wrestle with tough questions about when to help versus when to close struggling charter schools.

It is clear that school districts can't be trusted to work through all the problems of quality charter-school authorizers. Continued foundation investments in NACSA are necessary, as is a more aggressive effort to document the links between authorizer practices and the quality and stability of charter schools.

But government must also change its policy and make investments. With respect to policy, authorizers need to be held accountable, both for whether they create the opportunities for chartering and how responsibly they oversee schools once chartered. A multiple authorizers policy, allowing charter applicants to avoid hostile or negligent overseers, is a necessary sanction, especially for school districts. If others authorize successful charter schools, districts can suffer declines in the numbers of children they educate, and thus the numbers of teachers they employ and of schools they oversee.

State constitutions and No Child Left Behind also give states the authority to bypass or replace school boards that consistently neglect their obligation to provide effective education for all children. Buttressed by this authority, state education agencies can demand changes in district practices toward charter schools, and even dismiss school boards and arrange their replacement. Such actions are unlikely in today's public education system, where administrators all up and down the line are more loyal to one another than to the children and families served. However, these things can change under strong political pressures. These can be orchestrated by state charter school associations but are best delivered by foundations, businesses, and mayors who believe the futures of their communities depend on dramatic improvements in public education.

Authorizers also need funding for charter application approval and oversight of schools once established. Though some state laws allow authorizers to keep a tiny fraction of the money available to the schools they charter, most lack a clear source of revenue. Assuming that authorizers will be held accountable for performance, states need to fund charter authorizers as they do school districts, providing a fixed minimum amount for an authorizer that oversees even one school (e.g. the equivalent of one senior staff member and a clerk plus a small facilities allowance) with additional amounts for every school overseen. NACSA will develop models for authorizer operations that can be the basis for funding. None of them is likely to cost less than $150,000 for the smallest authorizer and $20,000 for each additional school overseen. This seems a hefty sum, but consider that under these assumptions, the New York City public schools central office would have a budget of about $22 million—a far cry from the hundreds of millions its activities cost today.

This is an area in need of both policy action and philanthropic investment. State charter laws need amendment both to give authorizers access to enough money to do their jobs effectively, and to allow charter schools to bypass inattentive or intransigent authorizers. Philanthropic investment in authorizer development—initially through expansion of NACSA's efforts—is also needed.

Table 7.1 summarizes the legislative changes needed in the states. As it shows, most states need multiple changes in their charter laws.

Table 7.1 Changes Needed in Charter Laws by State

Changes Needed In Charter Laws	*States*
Lift or eliminate caps on numbers of charter schools	Arkansas, Hawaii, Idaho, Illinois, Indiana, Iowa, Louisiana, Massachusetts, Michigan, Mississippi, Missouri, Nevada, New Hampshire, New York, North Carolina, Ohio, Rhode Island, Tennessee, Texas, Utah, Wisconsin
Equalize funding for students in charter and traditional public schools	Alaska, Arizona, Arkansas, Colorado, Connecticut, Georgia, Hawaii, Idaho, Illinois, Kansas, Louisiana, Minnesota, Missouri, New Hampshire, New Jersey, New York, Ohio, Oregon, Rhode Island, South Carolina, Texas, Wyoming
Create multiple authorizers and hold all authorizers accountable	All states
Direct state funding for authorizers	All states
Treat non-profits and for-profits equally	All states but Arizona, Colorado, Virginia, Wisconsin
Allow multiple schools under one charter	All states but Arizona and California
Eliminate fixed charter terms	All states

Infrastructure Needs

Small scale is a major problem for the charter-school movement. In a friendlier environment of policies and government oversight, the sheer numbers of charters would have elicited suppliers offering everything from real estate brokerage and building maintenance to accounting services, appropriately designed loans, management help and teacher training. A large charter sector would also naturally produce a cadre of former administrators, teachers, and alumni who understood what it means to work in a charter school and could adapt to them easily.

Regrettably, the factors working against scale for charter schools have also retarded development of this marketplace. Opponents can continue pointing to the marginal character of charter schools, the difficulty they have starting up, and their low but non-zero failure rates.

Thus there is reason to accelerate the development of a marketplace for the services and human capital that charters need. This will almost certainly require philanthropic investment, at least until the number of charter schools grows large enough to support needed services with school-paid fees.

Philanthropies are now making relevant investments in organizations capable of managing large numbers of schools in multiple sites. The firms thus created, called charter management organizations (CMOs), vertically integrate non-profit school providers that perform most of the roles of school districts. (Similarly structured for-profit educational management organizations (EMOs) depend on private investors rather than philanthropy.)

Such organizations are necessary, especially in an environment where opposition is strong and much of the intellectual and organizational capital required to run a school must be imported from outside a community. But EMOs and CMOs are complex and their central service and quality control mechanisms are expensive. A recent analysis of EMOs and CMOs by some of their major investors, including Gates foundation strategist James Shelton, concluded "such models are likely to grow slowly and in many cases are unlikely to be replicable at a broad systems level."[6]

If Shelton and his colleagues are right it seems unlikely that the existing EMOs, even with major foundation investments, can start enough charter schools in the next ten years to create charter-rich environments in a large number of localities.

One way to reach the benefits of scale is to concentrate the work of all the existing EMOs and CMOs in one or two major

6. Susan Colby, Kim Smith, and Jim Shelton, *Expanding the Supply of High-Quality Public Schools* (San Francisco: The Bridgespan Group, 2005).

school districts. The major actors in the charter movement, including associations, foundations, and CMOs/EMOs, should identify one or two mid-size cities willing to turn at least half their schools over to chartering, and develop these as demonstrations of what a fully-functioning charter system could accomplish. This would force a new level of collaboration among EMOs and CMOs, which now scatter their effort across very different parts of the country, from New York to Florida to northern and southern California.

An additional strategy, one that would complement rather than substitute for EMOs and CMOs, would be for pro-charter philanthropies to invest in local support infrastructures that would make it easier for new locally based charter schools to emerge. If new schools found it easier to secure facilities, obtain legal and financial services, and find teachers and administrators who know what it means to work in a charter school, wholly new charter schools could form more readily and successful schools would have a much easier time expanding and duplicating themselves. Individual charter schools with good reputations and more applicants than seats could reproduce as if by cell division, from one to two to four and so on. This could be done the same way that the Jesuits and other private school brands have expanded, by sending a few experienced people out to recruit others into a school whose core ideas the founders carry. School founders in new localities find the people and other resources they need locally.

The cell division model is different than the vertically integrated firm model used by the EMOs and CMOs, which control new schools centrally. It is not necessarily faster or more effective than the EMOs and CMOs, but makes greater use of grass roots initiative, and does not require an ever-larger central apparatus as the number of schools grows. However, it requires a far more friendly local environment, including policies and public oversight that do not stifle fragile new organizations, and access to talented educators able and willing to work in an entrepreneurial school setting. A local environment friendly to local charter school initiatives would also be a much easier place for EMOs and CMOs to operate.

Though a charter friendly local support environment would include many features, its two most critical elements would be schools' access to facilities and needed human resources. Charter schools often struggle for years to find adequate and affordable space, and virtually all new charter schools must overcome the fact that a high proportion of the teachers and administrators hired don't understand what they are signing up for.

The facilities problem is difficult both because charters have little money to put into rent—and unlike district-run schools any money they pay for rent reduces the amounts available to pay for instruction—and because safe and accessible space is often scarce in the neighborhoods that charter schools serve. The human resources problem is also difficult for two reasons: First, public school teachers and administrators, one important potential source of charter school staff, have learned all the wrong lessons about working in interdependent teams and accepting the natural consequences, good and bad, of their school's performance. Public school principals in particular often don't understand that they must run a productive organization and that managing on the basis of their favorite adage, "It's my way or the highway," isn't always the best way to run a school that adapts to students' needs. Second, individuals from outside the public education establishment often join charter schools in order to fulfill their personal visions of great education, but often find themselves in conflict with others who have similar motives but conflicting visions.

Philanthropic initiatives in a number of cities could help solve both these problems.

Charter schools' facilities problems could be solved, or at least ameliorated, by creation of local real estate trusts that specialize in locating facilities that might accommodate charter schools, making city lists of appropriate properties available to people interested in starting charter schools, helping potential charter school operators incorporate specific facilities plans in their charter proposals, and representing charter schools as they make lease agreements with private landlords.

Charter schools would find it easier to solve their human resources problems if there were larger numbers of teachers and principals who knew what it meant to work in a school that must attract and keep students if it is to survive. The numbers of such people will naturally grow over time, but in the short run there is a need for a deliberate effort to find and train people so charter schools can have a professional labor pool from which to draw. Formal training programs, whether offered by a non-profit or local college of business or education, could inform teachers about the difference between working in bureaucracy-run schools and schools of choice. Potential charter school teachers and administrators could also be taught the basics of budgeting, cost projection, obtaining insurance, hiring and personnel management, and management of contracts for services and supplies. Once hired these individuals would still have to learn about what makes their particular charter school unique, but they would start understanding the basic circumstances of work in a school of choice.

Willing state and local officials and pro-charter philanthropies could try out these ideas by experimenting with real estate and educator training programs in one or two cities. Ideally, these would be cities that have relatively few charter schools now, but the possibility of gaining many more due to need, room under state caps to permit formation of new schools, and the availability of local philanthropies and nonprofits capable of creating schools.

Neglect of NCLB's Chartering Provisions

No Child Left Behind requires school districts to create options including charter schools for children in consistently low-performing schools. At present, many districts are ignoring these provisions, and telling parents whose children are supposed to get options that there is nothing available locally. A few cities like Chicago have paid some attention to the options provisions, and are at least trying to increase the numbers of charter schools available.

Determined federal enforcement of NCLB options requirements would increase pro-chartering pressure. Federal officials need to keep the lost opportunities for chartering in mind as they try to placate NCLB's opponents.

Charter school associations in each state should monitor major districts' implementation of No Child Left Behind, pressing districts to provide charters as options for children in consistently low-performing schools.

For federal research sponsors and pro-charter think-tanks the first step is obvious. A national study of the gap between the numbers of children eligible for options under NCLB and the numbers of alternatives made available can illustrate the need for accelerated chartering. Then, state and local charter school associations could start demanding the opportunity to provide NCLB-required options, and local children's advocates can add their own demands on behalf of children left behind.

School districts might resist all these pressures, claiming that chartering is just one possible remedy that they are not obligated to use. These claims might need to be challenged in court. Though it is not clear that private parties can now sue school districts seeking the relief from bad schools contemplated by NCLB pro-charter, Congressional leaders could put teeth into the options provisions via a technical amendment giving parents private rights of action.

School districts are more likely to exercise an option that is a mixed blessing for the charter movement, reconstituting low-performing schools within the district's financing and collective bargaining systems, and calling them charters. In the past, district "reconstitutions" have been half measures that protect so many adult stakes that the resulting schools are little different than those that preceded them. Such half-baked chartering threatens to produce many bad schools, to the detriment of the children they serve and the reputation of chartering.[7]

School districts have the authority to charter in these ways but it is in the interest of the charter movement to make sure local school boards and local publics hear that half-baked chartering is not the only option. State charter associations should get onto local board agendas to say there is a right and a wrong way to do chartering and the wrong way will accomplish nothing. The "right" way must include giving charters real authority over hiring, firing, and spending, flexibility over use of time and materials, and status as schools of choice. State associations can also make sure local communities know about successful charter schools that could be imitated or hired to reproduce themselves, and about available EMOs and CMOs.

Summing Up

Taken together, the actions recommended in this chapter are ambitious and will be costly. They reflect our conclusion that the charter movement, though well started, is not likely to become a

7. For a discussion of the risks and possible benefits of chartering under No Child Left Behind, see Martin R. West and Bruno V. Manno, "The Elephant in the Reform Room: Are Charter Schools on a Collision Course with the No Child Left Behind Act?" *Education Week* 25, no. 34 (May 3, 2006): 44.

much larger factor in American public education—or even to be given a proper test as a system or mutually supporting institutions providing options for families—without serious efforts to level the playing field by elected officials, and continued investment in the capacities of schools, authorizers, teachers, and administrators.

How much action and investment, and for how long, are empirical questions. The barriers now reinforce one another, and actions that weakened each of them incrementally could lead to major expansions in chartering. However, chartering's opponents, especially teachers' unions and school boards, have been able to find and exploit weaknesses (such as ambiguous provisions of charter laws) that proponents had not anticipated. This is likely to continue. Charter proponents would therefore be naïve to think that the movement is close to some tipping point beyond which matters will take care of themselves.

Philanthropies have carried the charter movement to this point. It is time for elected officials and business leaders who want better schools, especially in big cities, to support the creation of real educational options. Charters need a level playing field, and only elected officials can ensure they get it.

Do the philanthropies need to continue supporting the charter movement? The answer is yes, especially if they take on the task of creating strong charter associations in every state, building up authorizers, and stimulating development of rich charter support infrastructures in at least a few localities. However, groups already created by philanthropic investment can also focus their efforts more effectively, especially on the federal level advocating for full use of NCLB provisions and in the courts.

After nearly fifteen years, the charter-school idea is an important part of the landscape of public education, but it is not as dominant or influential as some supporters hoped it would become by now. Relative to supporters' early expectations, the playing field has been tilted more sharply against charter schools than charter enthusiasts first understood, and creating large numbers of good new schools has proven more difficult than expected.

However, these difficulties seem large only relative to optimistic expectations. Despite opposition, the charter-school movement has grown faster, lasted longer, and held together longer than other reform initiatives like site-based management and magnet schools.

This is due in part to the fact that charter schools have bases of support outside the conventional school district structure. The private groups that run charters, foundations that fund them, and parents that rely on them sustain chartering against flip-flops in school board support and attacks from unions. This same support base also solves problems via investments in institutional support mechanisms and research and development. Thanks to foundation funding, chartering is one area of public education where research matters: problems get attention and dollars go to areas of evident need and opportunity. That sets chartering apart from other reform initiatives that were totally contained within the public-school system, which did not enjoy these forms of external support, and have consequently, languished.

Despite this extraordinary support, charter schools still face many challenges. Today's chartering policies let a few schools emerge but they prevent the growth of a critical mass of charter schools that could support one another, increase the numbers of teachers and principals who know how to work effectively in schools of choice, stimulate development of supportive vendors and financial institutions, and give parents many real options. We have suggested ways charter supporters—elected officials, advocates, philanthropists, and school providers—can work together on chartering's new frontier, which is the removal of barriers to scale and the development of mature charter sectors in key cities.

Contributors

Members of the Koret Task Force on K–12 Education

John E. Chubb, a distinguished visiting fellow at the Hoover Institution and member of the Koret Task Force on K–12 Education, is chief education officer and one of the founders of Edison Schools, a private manager of public schools, including many charter schools. Edison Schools today operates 130 schools in 19 states, with approximately 70,000 students. Chubb edited *Within Our Reach: How America Can Educate Every Child*, an assessment by the Koret Task Force, and is the coauthor (with task force member Terry M. Moe) of *Politics, Markets, and America's Schools*, a seminal work that argues for the introduction of free market principles within the American education system.

Chester E. Finn Jr., a senior fellow at the Hoover Institution, is chairman of the Koret Task Force on K–12 Education and president and trustee of the Thomas B. Fordham Foundation. Formerly a professor of education and public policy at Vanderbilt University, he also served as assistant secretary for research and improvement and counselor to the secretary of the U.S. Department of Education. The author of 13 books, he wrote, with William J. Bennett and John T. E. Cribb Jr., *The Educated Child: A*

Parent's Guide from Preschool through Eighth Grade. He currently serves as the senior editor for *Education Next.*

Paul T. Hill, a distinguished visiting fellow at the Hoover Institution and member of the Koret Task Force on K–12 Education, is a research professor in the Daniel J. Evans School of Public Affairs and director of the Center on Reinventing Public Education at the University of Washington. The center develops and helps communities adopt alternative governance systems for public K–12 education. His most recent publication is *Charter Schools and Accountability in Public Education.* He edited *Choice with Equity,* an assessment by the Koret Task Force, and he also contributed a chapter to *Private Vouchers,* a groundbreaking study edited by task force member Terry M. Moe.

Caroline M. Hoxby, a distinguished visiting fellow at the Hoover Institution and member of the Koret Task Force on K–12 Education, is the Allie S. Freed Professor of Economics at Harvard University and director of the Economics of Education Program at the National Bureau of Economic Research. She serves as a member of the Board of Directors of the National Board for Education Sciences. She is the editor of *The Economics of School Choice* and *College Choices.* She is also the author of several influential papers on education policy, including "Does Competition among Public Schools Benefit Students and Taxpayers," "The Effects of Class Size and Composition on Student Achievement: New Evidence from Natural Population Variation," and "Not All School Finance Equalizations Are Created Equal."

Paul E. Peterson, a senior fellow at the Hoover Institution and member of the Koret Task Force on K–12 Education, is the Henry Lee Shattuck Professor of Government and director of the Program on Education Policy and Governance at Harvard University. He is a member of the U.S. Department of Education's independent review panel advising its evaluation of No Child Left Behind and, in 2003, was awarded the Thomas B. Fordham Foundation prize for Distinguished Scholarship. Peterson is the editor in chief of *Education Next* and author or editor of numerous books on U.S. education, including *Choice and Competition in American Education, No Child Left Behind?: The Politics and Practice of School Accountability* (coedited with Martin R. West), *The Future of School Choice, Our Schools and Our Future . . . Are We Still at Risk?, The Education Gap: Vouchers and Urban Schools,* and *Earning and Learning: How Schools Matter.*

Other Contributors

Eric Osberg is the Vice President and Treasurer of the Thomas B. Fordham Foundation and the Thomas B. Fordham Institute. He is also a Public Affairs Fellow at the Hoover Institution. He is primarily responsible for financial and managerial issues at Fordham, and also works on policy projects related to school finance. Osberg earned a Masters in Business Administration and a Master of Arts in Education from Stanford University. He also completed a Certificate of Nonprofit Management as part of his MBA curriculum.

Brad Smith worked with Paul E. Peterson, researching the charter schools issue for the "School Choice in Milwaukee Fifteen Years Later" chapter in this book. He is a summa cum laude graduate of Harvard University's Department of Government. His research on Milwaukee's charter schools earned him Harvard's Thomas T. Hoopes Prize and the American Academy of Political and Social Sciences' Undergraduate Research Award. He currently lives in Chattanooga, Tennessee working on the United States Senate campaign of Bob Corker.

Nathan Torinus worked under Paul E. Peterson as an undergraduate honors thesis student at Harvard University in 2002–03, researching the school choice issue for the "School Choice in Milwaukee Fifteen Years Later" chapter in this book and for his thesis. He currently lives in Milwaukee, Wisconsin and works in the private sector, but remains interested in and active in the school choice scene in Milwaukee.

Index

EDUCATION next BOOKS

Education Next Books address major subjects related to efforts to reform American public education. This imprint features assessments by Hoover Institution fellows (including members of the institution's Koret Task Force on K–12 Education), as well as those of outside experts.

Assessments from the Hoover Institution's Koret Task Force on K–12 Education

Charter Schools against the Odds
Edited by Paul T. Hill
(published by Education Next Books, 2006)

Courting Failure: How School Finance Lawsuits Exploit Judges' Good Intentions and Harm Our Children
Edited by Eric A. Hanushek
(published by Education Next Books, 2006)

Within Our Reach: How America Can Educate Every Child
Edited by John E. Chubb
(published by Rowman & Littlefield, 2005)

Our Schools and Our Future . . . Are We Still at Risk?
Edited by Paul E. Peterson
(published by Hoover Institution Press, 2003)

Choice with Equity?
Edited by Paul T. Hill
(published by Hoover Institution Press, 2002)

School Accountability
Edited by Williamson M. Evers and Herbert J. Walberg
(published by Hoover Institution Press, 2002)

A Primer on America's Schools
Edited by Terry M. Moe
(published by Hoover Institution Press, 2001)